The Sons of Thunder

THE REAL TRUTH ABOUT PRISON MINISTRY AND THE MEN BEHIND BARS

Stacie L. Johnson

THE SONS OF THUNDER
THE TRUTH ABOUT PRISON MINISTRY AND THE MEN BEHIND BARS

Mark 3:17

James the son of Zebedee and John the brother of James, to whom He gave the name Boanerges, that is, "Sons of Thunder."

Christ calls whom he will; for his grace is his own. He had called the apostles to separate themselves from the crowd, and they came unto him. He now gave them power to heal sicknesses, and to cast out devils. May the Lord send forth more and more of those who have been with him, and have learned of him to preach his gospel, to be instruments in his blessed work. Those whose hearts are enlarged in the work of God, can easily bear with what is inconvenient to themselves, and will rather lose a meal than an opportunity of doing good. Those who go on with zeal in the work of God, must expect hinderances, both from the hatred of enemies, and mistaken affections of friends, and a need to guard against both.

(https://biblehub.com/commentaries/mark/3-17.htm, Matthew Henry's Concise Commentary)

Dedications

The book is dedicated to the faithful, talented, and resilient men and women of God that are behind prison walls pressing, pushing, and still standing strong letting their lights shine bright in dark places. To the returning citizens who showed the mockers and naysayers that they were wrong, you got out of prison and now you are successful, taking what you have been through and using it has a steppingstone and not a stumbling block. Be successful in whatever you put your hands to do! To the volunteers, employees and faith-based organizations who sacrificed their time, talent, and treasure to go behind prison walls to help set the captives free. To the families and friends of those who are incarcerated, for all your hard work, time and money spend year after year, and for your unrecognized loyalty, support and love to the men and women behind bars... if no has one ever said it, you are appreciated, and thank you!

To my team who took their time out to support the vision, those who did not mind going up the highway, walking behind razor wire, teaching, and preaching, thank you all so very much for your labor of love.

Lastly, I would like to thank my husband Frank who was part of the foundation and building of such a phenomenal vision. Thank you for allowing God to use your testimony to help others get free, and for being my rock and my support. Frank, I thank you for trusting me enough to enter a world that was dark and made for men; you knew God wanted to shine His bright light through me to set the captives free. I love you to the moon and back.

Jeremiah 1:5 *before I formed thee in the belly I knew the; and before thou came forth out of the womb I sanctified the, and I ordained thee prophet unto the nations*

John 1:12 *but as many as received him, to them gave the power to become the sons of God, even to them that believe on his name which were born, not of the blood nor of the will of the flesh nor of the will of man, but of God.*

For legal and privacy purposes, the names of the prison institutions are referred to by acronyms, and the names of certain inmates are referred to by their initials. The testimonies within this book were written by those directly involved with the Adonai Ministries and Family Is First Project.

It is the author's desire that readers will look past the slang and grammatical errors to see the heart of the men and women whose lives were forever changed by the transformational ministry that is The Family Is First Project and Adonai Ministries. Therefore, only basic editing was done to bring conciseness and clarity to the reader without threatening the integrity of the participants' voices or experiences.

Mrs. Stacie L Jonson M.A, CDCA, Ed.D Candidate
270 Northland Blvd # 209
Cincinnati, Ohio 45246

ISBN 978-1-734-1165-6-4

Table Of Content

Forward

"The Sons of Thunder," is another addition to your arsenal against the principalities and powers of dark places in this world. Pastor Stacie Johnson has made her footprint in a world with healing and deliverance in places where most think impossible. She has touched hearts and minds of the hardest of hearts with her sword. God brings light into darkness from these words of men and women who have felt defeated, overcome, and overrun with what seems impossibilities. Their stories will move you and realize there is truly a place of forgiveness in your hearts and place where we can all serve with the same passion of Pastor Stacie. Her sacrifice has not gone unnoticed, and the commitment to seeing those stripped of all identity receive their new identities in Christ Jesus. "The Sons of Thunder" is not a book but a memoir of strength and courageousness. Not only of the men and women she has shepherded, by faith as she continued to push through her own pain in triumph. Enlightenment will come from the many testimonies of God's goodness and breakthrough through this text.

Hope Williams Founder of Faith-Walker Ministries
Raleigh, North Carolina

Endorsements

To my anointed, beautiful wife Stacie, God has graced you to bless us with another powerful and empowering book that will set people free. I must say as your husband that God has truly spoken to you and through you to release another piece of yourself. Thank you for all your long hard days and early morning seeking God's direction in fulfilling His purpose in reaching people through your writing.

You have truly been an inspiration as well as a blessing to me and many others. May God continue to enlarge your territory as he continues to develop you in all areas of your craft. Know that through your obedience in writing this book, you will touch many lives, as well as giving the readers your truth that relates to the realities of prison and ministry which will impact many lives. Know that I'm your number one fan, and I support you all the way! I'm looking forward to the next five books that will be #1 best sellers. I love you and I believe in you.

Apostle Frank J. Johnson Jr

* * *

During my stay at the halfway house after repaying my debt to the state of Ohio, I met Apostle Stacie Johnson. This was a turning point in my life. Her clarity on self-evaluation and her direction on cleaning up internal issues that I was dealing with was phenomenal. Her point-blank real talk method hit me hard; and to meet someone in a broken system that cared was so refreshing that all of those protective walls you develop and immediately put up in prison somehow began to disappear after my second meeting with her.

The goals, dreams and self-expectations were renewed. Personally, I considered myself somewhat of a motivator and would ask myself who motivates the motivator. Well one name: Apostle Stacie Johnson. I've maintained a working friendship and, I would say, a client relationship with her for many years after my departure from the halfway house and I haven't looked back. She proved to me by actions, not words, that follow through, and dedication, too. As I said here real talk method works.

Fedel James

Introduction

It has taken me many years to place together all of my experiences about one of the most precious ministries that is near and dear to my heart; a prison ministry that was birthed from passion and my yes to The Most High God. You see, many people say they are called to prison ministry, but few want to count the cost of what it takes to not only start a prison ministry but to be consistent, disciplined, and faithful to the mission, no matter the cost and how tough it gets; and believe me, it will get tough.

This book is written to tell my truth about what it really takes to have a flourishing prison ministry that not only produces fruit but saves lives that have lasting results with the spirit of reconciliation

I would also like to share with you some special testimonials from the very men and women I have had the opportunity to mentor, lead and be a spiritual mother to. Some are still behind bars while other have been set free. It is these men and women who impacted my life as I went into the prisons to mentor, teach, and train them through my program known as Adonai Ministries and The Family is First Project.

These men dedicated and sacrificed their time and families, willingly entrusting me to reconcile them and bridge the gap in their relationships while being mentored and guided by me and my team. They sacrificed what they felt they knew to gain new knowledge and understanding on what it takes to be whole and become the real men and women God created them to be.

It is these men and women who took a stand and are still standing faithful serving God. Most of these men are still incarcerated while others have returned home to start their lives as returning citizens in their communities.

These are the sons of Zebedee, the Sons of Thunder! These are the men and women that stand strong behind prison walls waiting patiently, hoping, teaching, facilitating groups and mentoring the lost boys and girls who enter the dark gates of the prison world waiting to become men and women. This book will bring their world to your reality, and it will speak the truth about the extraordinary men and women that are hidden behind prison walls and what it takes to make a lasting impact on those who you desire to serve and see souls set free.

Matthew 25:40-45

And the King shall answer and say unto them, Verily I say unto you, Inasmuch as ye have done it unto one of the least of these my brethren, ye have done it unto me. Then shall he say also unto them on the left hand, depart from me, ye cursed, into everlasting fire, prepared for the devil and his angels: For I was an hungered, and ye gave me no meat: I was thirsty, and ye gave me no drink: I was a stranger, and ye took me not in: naked, and ye clothed me not: sick, and in prison, and ye visited me not. Then shall they also answer him, saying, Lord, when saw we thee an hungered, or athirst, or a stranger, or naked, or sick, or in prison, and did not minister unto thee? Then shall he answer them, saying, Verily I say unto you, Inasmuch as ye did it not to one of the least of these, ye did it not .

CHAPTER ONE

THE TRUTH ABOUT REAL PRISON MINISTRY

THIS IS A POWERFUL scripture because many people think that prison ministry is just for a select few, but if you really read the bible as the Holy Spirit gives some understanding, some of the most powerful people actually came out of prison. I have learned through many years of ministry and prison ministry that prison can be a place of torment; but it can also be a place that saves lives. At one time in my life, I thought like most people that nothing good could ever come out of a place that was designed for criminals.

Like most people think when it comes to inmates, they cannot be changed and there is no hope for them so why bother. Most people feel that when a person commits a crime, and they go to jail, that they are beyond saving and reforming; they lock them up and throw away the key. I'm here to tell you my truth about prison ministry and the men and women that are behind bars living saved lives, those people who are making an impact. I'm speaking about the unsung heroes who have been standing for years holding different ministers up with their prayers, supporting them from their 5 by 5 cells praising God in the midst of it all.

You see, my story was not developed from something that I read in a book or a research study that I conducted in college from looking at a bunch of numbers and statistics. My story is founded from the real experiences of traveling into the dark places of the prison world and seeing men and women in cages and ministering the Gospel of Jesus Christ to those whom society says were lost. It was my mandate to shine the light of love, knowledge and reconciliation and bring truth to the men and women behind bars that they could be the real men and women the Most High God created them to be in spite of their current state.

My purpose was to reunite them back with God and with their families because I found out through my own struggles that it is the family who are the biggest supporters, and they play the biggest roles, in their lives when it comes to rehabilitation and regaining their lives back into society. You might be wondering by now how I know about all of this prison stuff and where did I get all this information from?

Well, my journey started back in the early 90's, I was young in the Lord, newly saved and I was in the process of finding myself and tapping into to the gifs and talents God had placed in me. At that time, I was unsure of my calling and who I was, but I had a heart for God, and I loved Him. I was on fire, and I just wanted to do my part. At that time, my older sister who had been in church said that she had been praying and asking God where all the men where. She told me that God told her that they were locked up in prison and he instructed her to go into every prison and deliver one word to the inmates.

It has been many years, but I remember most of that word today. She said God was going to set them free, for those who kept their face to the wall just like Joseph in the bible, God was going to give them land that they did not labor for and churches that they did not build. It was a word for a specific group of men. When she got this mandate, she asked me if I wanted to come along and assist her. Well, I had always felt that sitting in the church building within the four walls was not for me.

I knew deep down that I needed something more; I knew that I had a greater purpose in life, and I was willing to take that big leap to find out what it was. I was scared, nervous and had developed my own idea about men behind bars and how they were hopeless cases, and trust me, people who have never gone into a prison, this is their first thought. Nevertheless, I pressed and decided to go. In the beginning we started out small, only local prisons, but then as we got popular, we branched out into other territories (prisons) in Ohio. They knew us as Philippi Ministries; it was three women with a purpose!

My sister did all the preaching, her friend Ms. Brown, who is now resting with the Lord, did all the praying and intercession and I was chosen to lead every single service. I was the one they put out first to set the atmosphere and MC. I was also the designated driver, so every prison we went to I got us there and made sure we got home. I took my position very seriously. For me, it was more than just driving, praying and being the master of ceremony, I was doing this for God, and he was using me. I wanted to make my daddy God proud. Back then, I had super-duper faith and I wanted to see Him move on His people. After many months of traveling to different prisons in Ohio and seeing how God was moving in the hearts of the men through our church services, we decided to have a bible study and invite some of the inmates to join us; you see, back then they did not have inmate email like they do now so we had to do it all through regular mail and who do you think was in charge of that? Yep, I was. We had about 15 inmates that we were corresponding with about the word of God. We never got personal with them because we knew and practiced being safe and having security measures in place.

Also, being three Black women, we knew that we had to have and keep our boundaries, as ministers of the Gospel this was highly important because of the stigma that is associated with women going into or working in a male prison. You see some women that have worked or volunteered in male prisons have ended up in sexual relationships with inmates. This bad reputation is, unfortunately, given all women who choose to volunteer or work in a prison, so we knew we had to show them different!

We had to be women of honor, virtuous, and strong in faith and character. We had to stand and not buy into the lie that all women who come into the prisons are looking for a man. Our prayer was that they see God and God is all they were going to get. Needless to say, this worked! God was on the move and so were we. Philippi Ministries toured to all the prisons in the State of Ohio, and we were well known for the anointing and the love, and the powerful preaching they received.

After a while they were requesting that we come back again and again. We did this for two years, but I could tell that things were changing with my sister; she was growing tired of it all and she was about to get married. Her soon-to-be husband did not like the fact of her going into a male prison, and he did not make it easy on her. I remember the day she called us over to her house and told me she was shutting down the ministry. I was speechless; devastated even. I had invested two years of my life and I was not ready to stop. My heart went out to all those men who were depending on us. I was crushed, but more crushed for them. I felt the burden on my heart and shoulders but there was nothing I could do because the ministry was not mine. She was about to get married and start her new life, continuing to go into the prisons was not in her plans. So, Philippi was no more, and I was stuck thinking about the last two blessed years of ministry from prison.

At that time, I had met the love of my life; he was incarcerated at the time and was very supportive and loving. I must say that he has always supported my call in God and stood by my decisions. During my dating and marrying process, I took a short break from prison ministry.

I really did not have a choice due to the ministry shutting down; but the burning desire to go back remained deep in my heart. After I married Frank, who was an inmate at the time in London Correctional Institution, I felt the pull even stronger to return to prison, only this time with my own ministry that God had given me. I was in prayer one morning at 5:30am and I heard the Lord tell me to name the ministry Adonai Ministries and this would be my prison ministry that would open the doors to the prisons for me.

Now you know I was all kinds of excited but scared at the same time because some chaplains knew me from being with the other ministry, and let me tell you, they were mad that Philippi had stopped for good. Some prisons would not let me back in because of that but I kept pushing and calling. I worked hard to convince them that I was not like my sister, and I was not going to drop them. I knew that I was in it for the long haul. Frank was very understanding, and he knew the call and anointing on my life; so, he cheered me on as I set out on my journey to build my team and go back behind bars; this time as Adonai Ministries.

As Adonai Ministries was forming, I spent a lot of time connecting myself with re-entry groups, attending The Department of Corrections functions, and collaborating with different organizations. I developed relationships with chaplains, directors, and community leaders because the vision God gave me for Adonai Ministries was more than just preaching and teaching. God showed me, after I attended a marriage seminar with Frank while he was incarcerated, that this was what he wanted us to do. That we were to teach the couples and families how to build their relationships from within the prison walls.

When I got that vision, I immediately ran home, called my mentor, wrote the vision down, tucked it away and worked on it. During the process of forming Adonai Ministries the Lord spoke to me and told me He wanted me to return back to school. You see, I was a high school dropout and school was not one of my favorite things. I was a hair stylist, and I had my own salon at the time. I was fine with my life, or so I thought. I was in church preaching, married, and to me things were ok. But God, when God has something greater for you, He will shake your whole foundation to get you moving.

God whispered in my ear one day that there was more to me than just hair and He wanted me to go back to school and get my degree in Criminal Justice because I needed the credentials for the arena, He was going to place me in. So, I set my heart to go back to school. I first obtained my GED and then I started working on my Associates degree in Criminal Justice. All the while, I was still building community relationships and fighting my way back into the prison system by sending emails, making calls, collaborating with faith-based organizations, passing out business card, building my website and securing the ministry name. This process was exhausting but I was up for the fight! I had a burning desire within, and a mission that I knew I had to fulfill. Being connected with Philippi Ministries showed me that the people behind bars are those who made some terrible mistakes in their lives, but they are our sisters, brothers, fathers, mothers, daughters and sons.

I learned not to view inmates in prison as, society says, "those people," but to see them as God sees them and they became just people, but a people in need, they became the lost population that society threw away and left for dead, believing that there was no rehabilitation or hope. I witnessed with my own eyes God change the hearts of some very violent men and women and I was determined to show the world that God can heal and deliver anyone. During this period, I knew I could not do this big task alone, so, I started connecting with people who I thought had the same vision and purpose as me. I knew I needed a team. I needed to have people holding my arms up and praying because I also knew the dangers and spiritual attacks I was about to face.

)

CHAPTER TWO

BEING A WOMAN ENTERING A WORLD CREATED FOR BOYS

Judges Chapter 4:6-7 *"The LORD, the God of Israel, commands you: 'Go, take with you ten thousand men of Naphtali and Zebulun and lead them up to Mount Tabor. I will lead Sisera, the commander of Jabin's army, with his chariots and his troops to the Kishon River and give him into your hands.'*

I LOVE THE STORY of Deborah because I watched a part of my life be mirrored to the scriptures in a way. You see, God told me that I was like Deborah many years ago when I first got saved and filled with the Holy Spirit; but I did not understand the prophetic word when it was given. It wasn't until I started walking some things out that I then knew the prophetic word was coming to pass in my life. God spoke to me and told me that I would lead many men to Him and into battle. I know this sounds crazy, and at that time I looked twice towards Heaven, looking at myself. I even asked God, "How can you send a little girl to do a man's job?"

That is when the Lord spoke and told me he does not look at the outer appearances of a person, but he looks at the heart, and because my heart was pure and I was a willing vessel, he was going to send me into dark places that most men would not go. So, I rounded up about six people and I started my quest. My first vision, or so I thought, was to develop a reentry program called the Gilgal Project. This name came from the experiences the children of Israel had in the wilderness on their way to the promise land. It represented the cutting away of the old and the development of the new.

So, I formed a board and shared my ideas; we typed up the paperwork and I thought I was on the move. I learned the hard way about business and being a woman in business; you see, some of the people on my team were men and I did not know it but deep down they did not believe in following a woman. These were men and women who had been affiliated with other outreach ministries, so I thought I was safe. I was real green and very trusting because back then I had tunnel vision and I believed that everyone wanted what I wanted, and that was to go behind bars and set the captives free. That was not the case after weeks of meetings and developing documents. I had one of the men tell me that he believed that the leader of the program should have some administrative skills. I was told that in order to lead, there are some things a leader must know; especially when it comes to creating documents and writing down the vision. You see, I had the vision, but I lacked the skills that would help me get to the next level, so I sought out people who I thought would help me.

Keep in mind that I was still researching going back to school and this was the icing on the cake that would push me into my purpose. I knew I did not have the skill set for such a big vision; but, when I heard this, it was presented in a way as if they should be leading, and the documents that were created had their voice and not mine.

I knew then that I had to do something quick, fast and in a hurry. So, I did the next best thing: I went out and purchased my own desktop computer. I was scared and anxious, but I knew it had to be done. I also purchased Windows For Dummies and MS Word For Dummies. I also taught myself how to type and how to format a document. This was very liberating for me as I was entering a world that was created for men. I felt my passion had to be told in my voice and I was determined to see it through. I was so excited, it seemed like things were pulling together. You see, at that time, I was unable to pay people for helping me and I found out the hard way some people are not always willing to volunteer their time no matter the cause.

The people on my team would assist with some of the tasks but when they felt they were done helping me, that is when my project plans would get delayed longer than I expected. Keep in mind I understood that people had lives of their own and I was not asking for a lot. Plus, I understood that this was my vision, so my drive was much deeper than theirs, back then I had a lot of zeal but not much knowledge in leadership and people took advantage of that. They knew I had the passion but lacked the skills to effectively lead. To be honest, I have never been a person who drags their feet, especially when God gives me a mission; so, I knew I had to learn and do it quickly.

I also learned that no one is going to run with your vision like you will! It was my passion, my call, and my vision, so I had to put in the work. Today, I have a whole new perspective on leadership and building teams. I know now that it's hard to grab a hold to a vision and run with it if you can't identify with it. I understand now that a person must first have a total understand and accept their own identity first, and then see themselves in the vision to run effectively. That person must also be willing to allow God to shift their mindset from what was to what will be.

If a person can't see it, it will be difficult to run with it. That is why **True vision** is seeing beyond with the natural eye and looking at life and situations with your spiritual eyes. Spiritual vision provides direction, it provides challenge and structure for life. Its understanding the divine purpose of God and recognizing your part in His plan. This is why the scriptures state in Habakkuk 2:2-3 ***Then the LORD answered me and said, "Write the vision and engrave it plainly on [clay] tablets So that the one who reads it will run.*** *For the vision is yet for the appointed [future] time It hurries toward the goal [of fulfillment]; it will not fail. Even though it delays, wait [patiently] for it, because it will certainly come; it will not delay (AMP)*

In the meantime, I still had a team of about five or six people. I had my friend help me with a power point presentation of all my notes and information about my program, now I felt we were ready to present it to the prison. So, I took the plunge and called WCI and set an appointment and took my team to the meeting. I was petrified sitting in front of the volunteer coordinator trying to explain what I wanted to do. All I remember from that day was this Caucasian lady looking at me through her glasses and telling me she was not interested in my program.

She said I did not have enough experience or information, so, she stated not at this time. Plus, she highlighted that I was a woman trying to come into a male institution and I did not have enough men with me. You know my feelings were hurt! I left their crushed and confused because I knew what God had said, but in my heart, I also knew it was time to go back to the drawing board. So, that meant more meetings and more revisions to the vision. Back then I had a husband-and-wife couple helping me, so I asked them for some assistance with the paperwork.

They seemed like very nice people, and they had the heart for what I was doing; or so I thought. I asked them to help me get a better perspective on volunteering and to help me fill in the gaps concerning my vision and what I could have been missing. I wanted the husband's opinion from a male perspective, so, trusting them both, I gave them my paperwork to view and work on. Sad to say they took my information and never returned. Keep in mind, years ago I was clueless about saving information on MS Word and using what was known back then as floppy disk to store information, so my precious power point and the information in it was gone!

Being who I am in the Lord, it was very hard for me to understand betrayal to that magnitude. I could not understand why they would not call me back or respond to my emails. I called for days, and days turned into weeks, and then it clicked. They were only with me to learn about my vision and get the plans of what and how I was going to operate inside the prison, so they could steal it from me. I felt so dumb and used for trusting them.

It made me feel like, because I was a young woman and alone, they could misuse me and take advantage of me, and they did. Keep in mind, I was dating a young man in prison and engaged to marry him. That part of my life I was not ready to share, so I was not totally alone; although, I was walking this particular journey alone, if you know what I mean. Nevertheless, I had to suck it up and rebuild my dream and start from scratch. With the desire still burning and the vision in my heart I set my eyes on the man I was to marry, who was incarcerated, and I spent my time nurturing that relationship while still connecting with faith-based organizations and attending seminars on re-entry. I wanted to learn all I needed to know about what would be expected from a wife of a prisoner.

Being a black woman attempting to go into a world that was designed for men was a very big struggle for me emotionally and mentally because of how the world stereotypes women in general. Feeling like this, I had to develop a thick skin real quick or fold and throw in the towel. But I was determined to prove them wrong and their views about women ministers. You see, even when I tried to call to get on the schedule to preach at some of these prisons, but because I was a woman, some of the chaplains requested my resume, or some even asked to meet me in person to get a look at me before they would let me come in. I have even been told by some chaplains, "You are a woman. What do you have to say to these men?" In spite of all the negative vibes, I kept on pushing because I knew deep inside of me, I had great purpose behind bars. I can even recall developing business relationships in the community and sharing too much of my information, thinking that I was making some lasting connections, only to watch those same people who had the funding and the teams in place go out and develop what I spoke out of my own mouth. It seemed like because they were men that they were able to move quicker than I did, and more opportunities were given to them; whereas, I had to push much harder and wait much longer. Needless to say, I kept in the fight in spite of what I saw and experienced being a black woman with a big vision. I remember expressing my hurts and concerns to my pastor at that time and will never forget the advice he told me. He said that being a woman in ministry will be a different experience than being a man in ministry. He said both (man and woman) will be placed in front of a brick wall and will be told to knock it down. He said that the man will be given a bulldozer and the woman will be given a toothpick and both are expected to do the same job. He told me just being who I am, that my road was already designed to be hard.

You see, growing up I dealt with very little racism, but I never had to deal with gender biases until I entered the corporate world and the Church. I counted the cost for attempting to go into a prison, but it never really dawned on me the cost I would have to pay being a black woman with a big vision. I also recalled my pastor telling me he did not know what to do with me because I was not like other women; He told me he had never mentored a woman minister (prophetess) before, and women were too emotional, all they did was cry all the time. I sat and listened to this man who was supposed to be my Pastor/shepherd and his male chauvinist attitude trying to speak into my life, and it was clear he was not equipped to train or cultivate the anointing that was on my life. He went on to tell me he could not train me or cultivate me in my calling.

Not too long after that I had no choice but to leave that ministry because I refused to die and waste away sitting in a church building and not being built up or developed in my call. But looking back, he was right about that brick wall and the tools given to me as a woman. I understood my battle, and yet, I was still willing to go if I had to use two shoestrings and a straw; I was going to get it done. By this time, I was married and Frank, my husband, and I had our own challenges to face. I was learning to be the wife of an incarcerated man while still taking care of home, working in my salon and on the ministry which would be our ministry when he came home. I endured many blessings and difficult moments as our relationship developed which I highlighted in my first book, "While You Wait." I talked about the stigma that goes along with loving someone behind bars. I discussed in the book how a lot of women do not like to share their experiences because of the embarrassment and humiliation they suffered.

There were no forerunners who were willing to take me by the hand and guild me; I made a lot of mistakes and most of them were financial. But the most important thing I learned was that the families had no voice! There was no programming available for Frank and me to glean from that would help us survive the prison life I chose. There was nothing in the community or prison that was developed that I could connect to that would help me connect with others who were living the life I also chose. That is when my vision became clearer: I knew that I had to personally walk down some dark paths in order to help others be set free. So, I started putting together a how-to-survive-a-prison-relationship manual for women. I know it sounds cheesy, but I had to start somewhere, right? I took my own life experiences and put them down on paper.

But this time, I did not tell anyone. I kept it tucked away because I learned from my previous mistakes of sharing too much with the wrong people at the wrong time; This time, I was able to tell my own story and using my own voice. I tucked it way and worked on it for months still believing that God was going to do great things. During this time, I was able to get back into a few prisons preaching on Sunday mornings and sharing the Gospel, but I knew God had a greater plan for my life and what Adonai Ministries was about to do.

I connected with a Pastor Maxine T who became a good friend of mine, and she believed in my vision and the anointing on my life. I shared some of my vision with her and she helped me put the pieces together as to how I would start. My heart went out to the families: the women who spent their money, gave their time, and sacrificed their lives to be caregivers of those family members who were incarcerated. So, I set my heart towards trying to gather them. Years ago, they had a company that had buses that would transport the women to the different prisons; the buses would pick them up at a local church and drop them back off later that day. This, I believe, was done a few days a week.

I recall sitting in the parking lot watching all the buses return and seeing all the women getting off the buses. I remember their faces to this day. They looked like a bunch of zombies carrying their babies and holding the little children by the hand. I saw no joy, there was no peace, and I surely did not see any love. What I saw was frustration, anger, and disappointment from a bunch of tired women.

I went back and expressed my concern to my Pastor Maxine that I wanted to form a women's group for those who were visiting the prison. So, I gathered my information, typed up my lesson and put together my binders. Pastor Maxine allowed me to use her building for my first meeting, and I was set. I printed my flyers and set off to go get those women! I remember waiting for the buses to pull in to drop them off from their long day of visiting the prison. My heart was racing, unsure about what I was going to say. All I knew was that I wanted to help heal the hurt they felt, so, I got out of the car and attempted to hand them my flyer with the meeting information on it.

Many of the ladies would not even look at me; they would not speak to me, and for those who did take the flyer, none of them showed up on the day of the meeting. I had a few close friends that attended my women's meeting to support; so together, we totaled about five women, and none of those women were from the prison bus. I was disappointed in the turn out, but I was told that I had some very good information, and the teaching was awesome. That part was encouraging but there was still that burning desire to help the families who were suffering internally; so, I went back to the drawing board, laying out my vision, revamping, and a lot of praying. I was still nurturing my relationship/marriage with Frank, and it was very fulfilling. As the years passed, I found myself becoming one of those women who spent most of her time being the caregiver of an incarcerated mate.

There were times I felt alone, abandoned, hurt, and lost. Many times, I felt judged for my decision to wait and love a man behind bars. There were many times I had to hold it all in due to the stigma that goes along with having and supporting a man behind prison bars. Sometimes, it was hurtful knowing the magnitude of the lack of support for families who give so much. You would think that entering a world that is as heavily populated as the prison system, there would be programming, groups, and community support; but it was nothing like that. I had to stand on my own, emotionally. I remember one of the most humiliating situations I had was when some so-called friends investigated Frank by looking him up just to see what he had done. Not because they cared about me but because they wanted to be nosey to find out the crime he committed. I was frowned upon by many, and I lost friendships, but through it all I continued to stay strong because I knew that God was going to use my pain and disappointment for his glory.

I knew he was going to use my joy and my strong bond He had formed with Frank and I to help others survive the prison experience. So, I pressed and endured. I loved it and I stayed in the fight. I started connecting with women who had husbands in prison that understood my walk. I had a very small circle of friends who supported my efforts, encouraged me, and prayed me through. I want to personally thank April, Vickie W, Marlene, Maria, Kelley, Mary, Tracey and Dennis, Kim C, Christina & Tye (who went home to be with Lord), Jenny and Willeta ("Wo" who also went home to be with the Lord), Vanessa, Vicky, Kim R, Kim C, Linette, and of course my beloved children Charles, Tyeisha and Tyrone. Please forgive me if I missed anyone, my apologies! These people were my rocks that held my arms up when I felt weary and tired.

They encouraged me, prayed for me, and listened to my venting. Again, I'm reminded of the scripture **Habakkuk 2:3** *"For the vision is yet for the appointed [future] time. It hurries toward the goal [of fulfillment]; it will not fail. Even though it delays, wait [patiently] for it, because it will certainly come; it will not delay. (AMP).* You see, God gave me the vision years ago, but seeing it manifest into full bloom took years. It was years of gaining personal and professional experience, knowledge, and endurance. It was a lot of praying and seeking God as he took me on this journey. I continued to minister on the pulpit and in the prisons preaching God's word, allowing the Holy Spirit to develop me as a wife and Prophetess.

I was in college studying for my degree in Criminal Justice and learning all I could about the profession that I wanted. One of my dreams was to open a halfway house for those men who were incarcerated for more than five years. My desire was always in the transition process. I remember working with this gentleman from another organization who was big into mentoring and reentry. I had the layout and blueprint; he had the connections and house. When we brought our minds together with what I thought would be a God explosion ended up being the same old scenario of, because he was the man, he thought he was supposed to take the lead, run the house, give the instructions, and set the rules. He thought I was only good for the blueprint and information. The issues were, I was not his wife, and this was not our home! He was confused on the roles and his small view of women would not allow him to see the bigger picture.

We were attempting to be business partners, needless to say that it did not workout, his narrow view of women was that we were only good for ideas and being the kitchen help, in addition to us not being able to get the proper zoning for the house the project never got off the ground. Looking back, I know God put that big roadblock up and I'm glad about! So, in all that extra drama I kept my main focus, and that was going to get these hurting women. You see, deep down I have always desired building relationships with women who were waiting,

I used to hear all the horror stories about the men who transitioned home and made a mess of their lives because there was no true transformation. Some of those men went back to prison while others lost their lives trying to repeat who they used to be, and others just destroyed their relationships because they were clueless about marriage, covenant and what it took to really be faithful to God, one woman and themselves.

I was determined not to end up like the others. I wanted my relationship with Frank to be all that God said it would be. But it would also be that relationship that people could model after and learn. You know, that point of reference to help couples see that this can be done. I was determined not to fail, so I pressed even harder. I ministered to these broke women who had been so mistreated and so misunderstood. I loved my husband unconditionally and I endured being a prisoner's wife while I continued to work on my vision, planning and revamping what I believed God was showing me.

My experiences as a prisoner's wife helped to mold my vision even the more. As the years passed, I continued to seek God and connect with community organizations that I believed would assist me while I pursued my journey. I recall taking small jobs with some community organization that delt with the prisons and reentry just so I could get a feel of the material and learn the basic business skills.

One day I was invited to a reentry meeting with my supervisor, while attending this meeting one of the ladies asked me a question, she wanted to know who I was and my experiences? When I shared my story, she was thrilled, and she said my story had so much weight and honesty to it she wanted me to be chosen as one of the people to help lead her project. While she was still talking my supervisor rudely cut her off and said in front of the entire group "I have been with this project for months! You come for the first time and open your mouth, telling your story and you are offered a position, this will not happen"! he was so upset that the lady gravitated to me and my story that he vetoed the very idea of me joining the board and working on the project.

Another job I took working for a non-profit organization, this position was in community outreach for a company called Project G. my job was to go around and try connecting church leaders to discuss community affairs and develop a software that would service the community's needs. I never knew that connecting church folk would be one of the hardest things to do and being a woman made it even harder. I needed the office experience, so I stuck in there. I remember I set up a meeting with one of the Pastors to explain my program.

I was very confident going to this meeting because I had heard great thigs about him, plus I heard he had some connects with the prisons and he had been inside the correctional facility preaching himself so I thought we will have a good conversation. When I got there, his assistant met me at the door, the young man was very kind, and I could tell he had a servant's heart. The pastor came in and he took one look at me and his whole demeanor shifted. I guess I did not look like I sounded on the phone. I took a deep breath and explained my program. I went on to explain my passion for prison ministry and how my husband was incarcerated and how he was fulfilling his pastoral call while in prison. I thought to myself "Why did I open my mouth", He did not let me get another word out.

This pastor ripped me up one side and down the other with his Harsh and hurtful words. He went on to tell me who do you think you are? He told me that my husband was NO pastor being an inmate, as he turned his nose up with the angry frown. He went on to tell me that he has been on the battlefield for years and who do I think I am to come in his church acting like I'm going to save the world! After he openly humiliated me, he stormed out of the room. I was left in the room shocked, unsure, vulnerable and clueless as to what had just happened. His assistant came in with a heartfelt apology, he must have heard the whole thing and I could see the embarrassment on his face. He went to try and explain to me how much of a good man is pastor was, His assistant said, "he just has a little issue with women". My thoughts were, "Just a little! and this is what I have to face? At that point I did not want to hear another word. I had seen, experienced, and heard enough, I wanted to get out of there.

When I got back to my office, I told my supervisor what happened to me and I broke, I cried like a baby because I had never felt so violated and humiliated like that, and the fact that he was a pastor made it even worse. At that point my supervisor quickly took on the father role and schooled me about businessmen and pastors and what I needed to do if I was placed in a situation like that. He told me to never let another man emotionally rape me of my self-esteem and womanhood that I was more valuable than that.

Well, I guess you figured it out, neither of those positions last, they were just steppingstones to where God was taking me. I know now that I had to experience first had the hate, the criticism, the biases, the spiritual attacks, and some disturbing events for this ministry of being called into the prison world. When people tell me that they have a prison ministry, I just chuckle within myself then I ask them do you really know what it's going to take.

You see people want impact, they want anointing, they want a big name, but most people are not willing to suffer, they are not willing to do whatever it takes to reach that goal. I wish I could tell you that ministry can happen overnight but that would be farthest from the truth. True prison ministry takes blood, sweat, tears and lots of prayer. It takes time to develop and time to grow. I thank God that I never gave up because not too many people live to see the fruits of their labor!

CHAPTER THREE

THE FAMILY IS FIRST PROJECT

TEN YEARS HAD PASSED, and it was time for Frank to come home. My vision was safely tucked away as I continued to work on it, plus learn my new role as a wife. I remember those moments like yesterday, seeing him walk out of that prison door for the last time, sharing our first ride home, meal, date etc. What I could never shake was the prison experience that laid the foundation for where we are today. I must say, back then in 2005, things were much different. I think with the programming and community support, they were just learning that rehabilitation was a must because the recidivism rate was on an all-time high. I remember a lady telling me that I was going to have to be my husband's re-entry.

I did not understand what she meant at the time but when he came home it was clear about all the stressors he and I would have to endure just in the transition from prison to home. I learned very quickly that the family was the key! I tried reaching the families in the community, but it did not work, so I asked God how do you want me to do this? I heard him say that I was going to have to go back in the prison but this time I'm taking my experience as a prisoner's wife and my education and community experience with me. God kept reminding me what he told me in His word:

"The Spirit of the Lord GOD is upon me; because the LORD hath anointed me to preach good tidings unto the meek; he hath sent me to bind up the brokenhearted, **to proclaim liberty to the captives, and the opening of the prison to them that are bound (Isaiah 61:1)"**.

God told me that this was my mandate and to go and set the captives free. Frank and I were both in agreement, and to be honest, because he was an ex-mate and a man, they jumped at the opportunity of having him come back in. So, I set out on a mission, but this time I had my husband at home; he agreed with me, and the timing was perfect. The first step was to add him to the volunteer list at the prisons which I was already affiliated with through preaching. I had built a good reputation and relationships with the chaplains, so it was not hard to get him added. I continued to work on my vision but now it became clear what God wanted me to do. That is when I changed the name of the vision from the Gilgal Project to The Family is First Project. Now I had a firm foundation upon which the vision could stand. The Family is First Project was initially created for those couples who had incarcerated mates in need of emotional healing and relationship support.

26

It was designed to assist those relationships in breaking down the communication barriers; to help both the man and woman cherish what they had, and most of all, to teach them how to deal with doing time while building and cultivating their relationships. I was ready! I sat down at my computer and began to type, and this time, it started to flow. I typed up the proposal and I contacted WCI and told them what I wanted to do. Things were a little different at WCI. New faces emerged, which worked out for my good. I talked to the volunteer coordinator who scheduled an appointment for me to come in and talk to the Warden. I could have dropped the phone because it seemed much easier than the last time, there were no hindrances, no fears, and no insecurities; and this time I went alone. I did not have a team. All I had was God. So, I met with the warden and the volunteer coordinator. I was a little surprised because they were two African- American women in powerful positions. Seeing this was rare and I appreciated just being in their presence.

They listened to my story and what I wanted to do, and they were sold! From that point, we scheduled the days that Frank and I would come up once a week and speak to the couples. We created flyers that would be passed out in the dorms, and for those who were willing to attend, they would have to send a message to the volunteer coordinator. At first, I was expecting a room full of men because I saw how great the need was. It turned out I was limiting myself, initially making it a re-entry program for those men who had one year until they returned home. Unfortunately, we did not get anyone to respond.

I found out that there were not that many men who were close to going home or married, so, we revised the admission rules and opened the program to men who were in a relationship; to those who wanted to grow as a couple and learn how to deal with having a prison relationship. After we put this flyer out, we had about 10 couples who signed up. We were off to a good start! Excited and ready to roll, we had a date to go in, and now it was time. The scary part to all of this is that I had the proposal, but I had no material! What was I to do? Wednesday morning was the set days but what were Frank and I to teach on? Where do we start? I had these people showing up and now I have to get prepared. Well, being that it was time to use what I had learned over the years, and first things first, I created multiple forms and decided that the first class would be an orientation class signing confidentiality forms, consent forms and rules and regulation forms.

I also got a list of the inmates who would be attending the class so I could pull their profiles offline and pray over them, and to also get a feel of who was entering the class. This worked out well because it gave me a lot of background and information about the couples we were about to teach and minister to. Once the orientation was over and it was time to start the classes, every evening the day before the class the Lord would download to me what he wanted us to teach. I would sit at my computer and type for hours as the Lord would speak in my spirit. You see, it was strange because we had to go inside the prison to get the men and then they would convince the women to participate. So not only were we on the inside teaching and training the men, but the prison would also allow the wives to come in and get taught with the men once a month. I also developed extra meetings in the community for the wives and girlfriends.

We would meet monthly and talk about their prison relationships and how they could take care of themselves in the process of being a caregiver to their loved ones. The Family is First Project for couples started out as a 6-month process every Wednesday morning at WCI, and the women met Saturday morning, once a month. It was a true blessing. We had a total of 10 couples starting out; we discussed topics like feeling lonely but not alone, communication, how to fight fair, and much more. Back then we had the only program that was operated from inside the correctional facility by a black woman and her ex-inmate husband, plus having groups sessions with the wives in the community. It was exciting and very challenging for me because each Tuesday night as I prepared for class, the Lord would download what he wanted us to teach, so I was creating materials weekly. Frank and I met some really solid couples who are still together to this day. You will get a chance to hear from some of these men later on in the chapters to come; it was these very men who helped to deposit in me a strength that I never thought I had.

Because of all of my past hurts and fears, I was very unsure about teaching, facilitating and speaking to large crowds. God used the Family is First Project and the men behind bars to help me develop in my skills of adding value to others, public speaking and facilitating large group in a special way. Frank and I watched these couples grow through leaps and bounds; we connected not just as their facilitators but as their pastors and lifelong friends. By this time, Frank and I were both going into the prisons preaching the word of God and developing our own ministry.

We were getting to be pretty well known in the prisons because of him being an ex-inmate and me spending many years preaching within the prison walls and being known as the wife who waited for 10 years for her husband to come home. The Family is First Project couples was growing fast with each lesson, but we only still had 10 couples. The part that was always difficult to process was that some of these ladies were doing a life sentence with these men. I learned early on that the hope of a man does not depend on how much time he has to do behind bars because hope is hope!

The men that were doing life sentences had the same hope and similar struggles as a man that was doing 5 to 10 years. Most of the men in our class were high profile cases but we treated them all the same. It did not matter to us what they had done, Frank and I never came in looking through judgmental eyes.

Once they were approved to be in the class and I pulled their profile, I prayed over it and left it at the altar with God! Through our prison experiences, Frank and I both had lots to deposit and share. This was our opportunity to be transparent about our relationship to an audience that understood and was willing to grow from what we had endured. At the end of our six-month sessions, we had arranged with the prison to allow the wives to come in and celebrate with the men. We had a small graduation ceremony where the prison allowed us to bring in food and treats as we celebrated the success of the couples. Because of it being a prison and the high-profile cases in the class, we were restricted from taking some photos. The families were allowed to take pictures and give them to us be we could not bring our camera or post any information on our webpage.

Frank and I did this for two years, teaching the same couples and putting out the same flyers, but we were not getting a big response like we thought we would, seeing that the word was spreading. On the outside, our lives were beginning to shift. I was working a 9 to 5 and Frank started to work harder doing contract work rehabbing houses, plus his special needs daughter, Franquie (who has gone home to be with the Lord), had come to live with us. This shifted our family situation a lot; but we kept pushing towards the vision God gave. With the home changing and life happening, we still managed to block out Wednesday mornings for The Family is First Project. By this time, our ministry was growing, and we had people within the ministry that wanted to help. This helped to lighten the load, but this required that we train and orientate them. Nevertheless, we pressed toward the vision.

Our Beginnings

Zechariah 4:10 *Do not despise these small beginnings, for the* LORD *rejoices to see the work begin, to see the plumb line in Zerubbabel's hand."*

CHAPTER FOUR

THE GAME CHANGER, FROM COUPLES TO FAMILIES

I T WAS THE THIRD YEAR of the Family is First Project when my life took a dramatic turn. As we were planning to start our new class, we sent out flyers to all who desired to participate, but this time, we did not get a great response. You see, the wives and inmates that had been with us for two years were now considered alumni families and these inmates had now become our eyes and ears in inside the prison. They were our advisors on how to gather extra men into the program. So, we put our heads together with the volunteer coordinator Mrs. P and we decided to open up The Family is First Project to everyone. The only restrictions were that you had to have a family member who was actively visiting, and they had to be willing to participate.

37

Plus, you had to be ticket free for at least 3 months which meant you could not have been in any trouble or had a violation for contraband, violence etc. When we did that, the response was amazing! We had over 40 men apply, and the volunteer coordinator did a very good job of weeding the ones out that she knew were not serious. You see, there will always be those men and women who do not want to do right, they just want to take advantage of programs just to get out of their cells. So, working with the volunteer coordinator and the men that were with us for two years that really loved the program, we knew who really wanted change and who were just playing. We all agreed to accept no more than 25 men which added up to 25 families.

The prison agreed to allow the families to come up for an orientation session by themselves to learn about the program. This took place on a Saturday morning inside the prison visiting room. It was amazing to see so many family members show up at 8:30 am in the morning excited, scared, not sure but willing to listen. The ice breaker and opening speech I gave before I talked about the program was of me telling my story and the things that I had to endure and suffer being the wife of an inmate.

I was very transparent about the good, the bad and the ugly. When talking to the families I made sure I left no stone unturned. Needless to say, there was not a dry eye in the place. God used me to prick the hearts of the families. He used me to enter into their darkest world of pain and hopelessness to shine a light of hope on their situations. Once I explained about the program and what their roles were, they were all in. Then Frank and I met with the men, and we orientated them. It was at this time that Frank told his story about his prison experience; the men were all kinds of excited.

We were ready to roll. By this time, I had enough material that I did not have to develop much more; but I did have to revise some things now that the program had gone from being a couple's thing to a family thing. I realized very quickly that prison was not just about girlfriends and wives, but it was about the friends, mothers, daughters, sisters, and wives who were spending their money, sacrificing their time, listening to and putting up with all the inmate and prison drama that was attached.

These family members were mostly women like me who were cut from another cloth, and that cloth was thick skinned, compassionate, loyal, and believed that people could change. Along with the men who you will meet later, I want to personally thank all the women who have waited and sacrificed everything for the one they love, whether it was a son, father, uncle, or husband. I honor you and I thank you for allowing both Frank and I to pour life back into your souls and bring hope and restoration.

You might be wondering where the husbands and fathers and brothers of these inmates were. Well, back then, starting out, it was hard to get any man to come into a prison because men view prison differently than women. I learned that fathers tend to blame themselves, and also felt that if their sons do the crime, then they need to do the time by themselves. While women, on the other hand, will care for you and come see about you no matter what. This was something I prayed about as we continued to have class. It took a few years for our prayers to manifest, and when it did, we had fathers and brothers attending the meetings. Sons were reconciled back in relationship with their fathers, the barriers of communication were destroyed, and you could see the sudden changes in the lives of the families.

Looking back, The Family is First Project started in March 2007 and operated through 2008. It was around 2009 when my life took a dramatic shift. In July of 2009 my daughter, Tyeisha, was diagnosed with Non-Hoskins Lymphoma which they said was an aggressive type of cancer. At that time, Frank had decided not to continue with going into the prison to facilitate the program with me; it had become too stressful. He, himself, was still adjusting with returning home and working.

During the time when Tyeisha was about to have surgery to remove her gall bladder, that evening (after her surgery) Frank and I were ordained as pastors of Ebenezer St. Mark Church in Dayton, Ohio. This was a very trying time for our family. I spent many nights in the hospital with her even to the point of traveling back and forth from Cincinnati to Columbus where she was staying at the James Cancer Hospital. I would travel to WCI on Wednesdays to teach my class and then travel to Dayton on Sundays to preach or support Frank with the church. The Holy Spirit did send a wonderful couple to me to help sit with Tyeisha when I had to travel. They prayed for me and held my arms up when I felt weak. I want to acknowledge Prophet James "Dad" Mosley and Alise Mosley for their love and support. Also, God had blessed me with a wonderful friend who came and sat, sung and prayed with my daughter. I want to also thank TaKeesha for all her love, compassion and faithfulness, Vickie and Wiletta for being there through the long hospital stays. In July 2010, my only daughter, Tyeisha, lost her battle with cancer but gained her wings, her new life with the Lord. I knew that letting her go had so much more to do with me then her.

I watched God do miracle after miracle in her life and I was not about to stop in my vision because I knew God had given me a strength like no other. If anything, losing her pushed me deeper into my purpose of seeking God and totally depending upon Him for guidance. We continued for a short while to pastor in Dayton until we both heard the Lord say it was time to move on. You see, we learned the hard way that you have to work as a team and the biggest part of ministry is that we all have to walk in agreement. Amos 3:3 states, ***"Can two walk together, except they be agreed?"*** It was hard for us being new pastors without guidance and support from the overseer and church team. We did not have what is called "spiritual parents," so we had to learn the hard way and that was how we functioned alone!

When we decided to leave, it was God's perfect timing, and back I went to WCI; but this time, I was doing it by myself. Keep in mind that the men who had previously started with us had invested their time and their hearts, now they were considered the alumni and my faithful advisors. We conducted meetings on how the program was running and what I could improve on.

I took lots of mental notes and honored the fact that they were willing to follow a woman no matter what! They supported with their heartfelt love and honor plus, The Family is First Project was like no other program they had ever been connected with, so they were willing to give their all. They knew that we were about to make history and the vision was a pot of gold just waiting for the taking. Appreciated them then, and I still do today!

I also used to call them my personal bodyguards because they were true watchmen on the wall, standing guard in the spirit against the enemies who tried to lurk and infiltrate into the program to bring disruption. I can't recall any chaos in the program because those men who did not have the right motives where always shut down immediately and weeded out.

Romans 8: 35

Who shall separate us from the love of Christ? Shall trouble or hardship or persecution or famine or nakedness or danger or sword? As it is written: "For your sake we face death all day long; we are considered as sheep to be slaughtered." No, in all these things we are more than conquerors through him who loved us. For I am convinced that neither death nor life, neither angels nor demons,[b] neither the present nor the future, nor any powers, neither height nor depth, nor anything else in all creation, will be able to separate us from the love of God that is in Christ Jesus our Lord.

CHAPTER FIVE

THE STRUGGLES OF CHANGE AND COMMITMENT

OPENING THE Family Is First Project to the families was a huge step, it required lots of work, discipline, and commitment. I knew I had a long road ahead, but I was willing. Plus, I had this burning pull inside me that people could change. I was driven by a desire that was developed deep within my soul. By this time, I had a couple of people who were standing with me. I want to give Mrs. P and April a big shout out because they were there in the beginning. She saw all the sweat and tears of making the Family is First Project great.

So, Mrs. P and April, thank you so very much for all your hard work, consistently, and labor of love! Our first family session with the men was jam packed and awesome! We had over 25 men plus the alumni who attended to observe, support and add their own experiences. In these sessions God allowed me to dig deep into the hearts and minds of incarcerated men, and with the Holy Spirit, set them free in their minds. You see, I am a firm believer that bondage is a mindset; it does not matter if you are walking free on the streets or in a prison cell, if your mind is held captive to the enemies of your past or present hurts and fears, you will forever be a prisoner. So, I taught a lot of cognitive behavior therapy (CBT) which I learned when I became a case manager working for a local halfway house.

You could say that I was double-dipping because my day job was managing ex-offenders who were transitioning back into society. I facilitated alcohol and drug groups, sex offender groups and CBT groups. I had a caseload of 35 to 65 men depending on how we were staffed, but I made the best of it. I took those skills and made full use of them on Wednesday mornings as I facilitated the men and their families in the prisons. As I grew in my craft and gifting, the men did not make it easy, the more they grew, the more I was challenged to go higher in my knowledge and learning.

I had always had a prayer life, but it seemed like I stayed on my face even more because now I was accountable for so many souls. I knew the cost and I was willing to pay it because I was seeing the growth and the change happen right before my eyes. Looking back, I know God provided. I did not have much money; I was working a 9 to 5 to fund the ministry; we were living on a tight budget.

And with Frank only being home a few years, we were still adjusting ourselves. I continued to teach and facilitate the men and their families, watching them flourish and open their hearts to healing and communication for total growth. We had even worked it out with the prison to have a family day of worship where the families were allowed to participate in a worship service with the inmates in the break room once a quarter on a Sunday morning. It was off-the-chain anointed! I remember having praise and worship and preaching to a broken population of people who wanted to be healed, this lit a fire under me to push harder. This drove me even more because it's one thing to preach or teach to a people who appreciate your anointing and are hungry for change opposed to a people who are too religious, churched and stuck in their own ways and don't want to change.

I'm not judging, but I have been in many arenas and my prison experience has been one of the best because of the authenticity of the hearts of the people. They have nothing else to lose. They were thorough in their approach to God and serious about changing their lives and relationships. The part that was most challenging for me was digging deep into the hearts of these men and holding my stance in God. Deep down I knew that there was some who questioned my leadership abilities because I was a woman, but not just any woman. I was a young black woman, and I was easy on the eyes. Some would consider me to be beautiful. I never wanted my beauty to get in the way of what God wanted to do through me, so I had to be virtuous, strong, anointed and committed to God, my husband, and my call. I always desired to show my intelligence, pure spirit, and love for God more than anything. During my teaching moments in WCI, I would always keep in the back of my mind the negative words that people spoke about my vision.

It's funny because it gave me a push to prove them wrong and a greater desire to see God move. I recall back in the planning process of the Family is First Project, I sought advice from a guy I knew who had been in prison. He was an acquaintance and we had been affiliated with a reentry group in the community, so, I thought he would be the best one to give me advice. I was wrong. I told him what I wanted to do, to go into the prisons and teach the men and their families. He basically told me that because of how I looked, and being a woman, they wouldn't take me seriously. He told me that they would only come to see me because I was a woman, but would not hear what I had to say and would openly humiliate me. For the record, I refused to believe a word of that nonsense! I left the meeting a little disturbed. Not because I believed what he said but because this is how some men/people really think and feel about women ministers.

There were a lot of people who wanted my program to fail because I was a black woman entering into a man's world to bring change. There was a big part of me that wanted to prove to the men in the community who were judging me that they were wrong. I wanted to show them and other women that God could do anything and that beautiful women have brains and skills too! I was determined to be known for my anointing, godly character, educational and corporate skills and not just another pretty face. So, I dug deep in God and in my studies and I learned, and I prayed, and I continued to press into my vision. It was full speed ahead! I knew entering a world that was designed only for men was going to be challenging, and sometimes hurtful, because of how women in general are viewed by some. Let's be real, some men/people think women are catty crybabies with their emotions all over the place.

They look at us as weak objects who are only good for sex, cooking and teaching bible study in the churches. So, if you were nice to look upon, most would not take you or your call seriously, I guess. I knew that I was coming up against the odds, but I also knew that the odds were in my favor because I had the Most High on my side and I was determined not to fail! I did not care what they thought, and I did not hide my beauty. I went in virtuous, strong, and the beauty of the Lord was my garment, and I was well received. When the men saw me, they saw the love of God. They saw a woman who was no nonsense, straight no chaser, loyal and faithful to God and her husband and about her business, determined to set some people free.

All awhile I honored my husband even though he was not present; I talked about him all the time; so, for the new guys and families who came into the group, they knew Frank through my testimonies and how I honored him. I knew that I was not just building and pushing for myself, but I was building and pushing for all the men and women who would one day follow after me. Those men and women are called by God to lead a troop, those who would have a big vision ad are willing to run in seeing the lives of individual transformed!

John 12:32
And I, if I be lifted up from the earth, will draw all men unto me. (KJV).

"You never change your life until you step out of your comfort zone; change begins at the end of your comfort zone." Quote -Roy T. Bennett

CHAPTER SIX

BUILDING UPON A SHAKING FOUNDATION

B Y THIS TIME, the word had started to spread about the program and each year we would have more men and families joining. We had gotten to be so big that I knew it was time to start developing people to help me facilitate these classes. So, I began training people in my local church and other ministries. I must take the time out to acknowledge for a moment those men and women who came behind bars and or assisted with Adonai Ministries and The Family is First Project: Willeta, April, Christina, LaTesa, Lora, Tyra, Delisa, Linette, Hope, Tonya, Chantell, Chris, Loretta, Katina, Perce and Michelle, Cheryl and Carl, Fedel and Tonya, Isaac and Gretchen, DeRon, Stephanie, and most of all, my husband Frank.

I want to personally thank each and every one of them for their hard work, for taking out their time, and for their dedication to seeing lives changed. Thanks for supporting the vision. As the classes grew the celebrations became bigger and bigger. Each year, we would acknowledge each man for their hard work and commitment to the program. We celebrated them for their change, growth, commitment, family reunification and transformation. Each man was awarded a certificate of completion, and I had a few of those men give speeches and word of encouragement to the families. We had some rap, and even recite poetry. Some of those spoken words and speeches you will read later.

It was phenomenal to see these men be transformed. And not only that, to watch them put the work in and see the shift in the mindsets. I can be honest, there were times when I doubted my ability and I wanted to quit; but then I would go inside the prison and listen to the men and see the participation, transition, and change. Those were the times the Lord reminded me of His word and who and what He has called me to be, and this was my encouragement and charge of strength that I needed to press on. As much as I thought I was teaching them, they were also teaching me! I thought I was a strong black woman already, but as I was teaching and training these men, I leaned to push past my fears, dig deep into vision and go directly for the heart. Let's be honest, I had entered a world of darkness, brokenness and fear. I entered a world that was initially designed and shaped to tear down the spirit of a man; a world that was set to reprogram and encage the body and the mind until the individual breaks. But God! He sent me with the love and the spirit of reconciliation to help pull these men and women out of dark places in their minds and hearts, and even the prison staff was starting to notice the change.

There were times I would come into the prison, and while I was checking-in, the guards would acknowledge my level of commitment and the awesome job that I was doing and how they saw a difference in the men's attitudes and behaviors. This not only encouraged me, but it was a blessing that they saw God working. And to be honest, some of the guards adjusted their schedules to Wednesday morning so they would be the ones monitoring my class because they were being touched as well by the teaching, they wanted to be in an atmosphere that fostered real change, and the presence of the Lord was always present. As the classes grew in numbers and anointing, I continued to preach behind prison walls.

When the men in the class knew, I was coming to preach on Sunday morning, they would all attend and pack the house! Oh, what a time in the Lord we had! The worship was always so moving, and the word was rich and powerful and many, many men gave their lives to Christ., I did not realize then but to most of them I became their Pastor. They looked to me for spiritual guidance. By this time, I was preaching at places like Warren, Lebanon, London, Madison, Lorain, Marion, North Central, Dayton, Lucasville, and Ohio State Penn. Adonai Ministries was on the move and God was taking us higher in Him each time we ministered. We had gotten to be so big that I had to set up two different teams: one for The Family is First Project (the teaching and facilitating) and the other team for Adonai Ministries (traveling and preaching inside the prison).

Most of the experiences that I've had preaching in the prisons were unbelievably phenomenal and a blessing, but how many of you know when the spotlight starts to shine on you, the enemy is also watching and waiting. I want to briefly share some of those experiences; I want to take you into the world behind bars, the blessing and anointing that people don't get a chance to talk about and share. In this book, I am making public the hidden miracles that went unspoken. I remember a certain service at WCI when I took my team in on a Sunday morning and my spiritual daughter Apostle Chantell had preached a powerful message. During the altar call, people were bringing me men to pray for.

There was a young man in the crowd who was bought to me, and as I laid my hands on him and began to speak into his life through the Holy Spirit and my Prophetic office, I sensed this man was powerful and had a lot of influence in the camp. But I also knew that God wanted him saved and delivered, so, I dug in praying for him, calling Pastor Chris over to assist me. As we were praying for this young man, he began to shake violently; his eyes rolled back into his head and the spirit of God was all over him.

He fell back on floor and while my catchers laid him down as he shook, he was levitating off of the floor. One of the inmates who was playing the drums during the worship could not believe what he saw. He stood up and threw his drumstick under the man that was levitating to make sure he was not seeing things. As we continued to pray for him as the Holy Spirit was moving on him, I felt led to start praying for the other men, so I left him there while a few of the team and inmates attended to him and the rest of the team assisted me in praying for others. When he woke up his very words were, "What did you do to me?"

He repeated it over and over. My response was, "Nothing. It was God." This young man burst out in tears as the men gathered around him to show their love and support. The other young man who threw the drumstick got saved that day! God showed up and showed out!!! When I returned to the prison the following week, the news had spread all around the compound about me and what had happened. Upper management had also heard about what was taking place on Sundays when me and my team were coming in. I was told by some of the staff that I needed to be careful because some people in upper management don't understand the move of the Holy Spirit, so I should tone it down a bit. And from that point, I was told I was not allowed to touch the inmates when I prayed.

I acknowledged, respected, and heard what they were saying, and I and understood that I was a woman in a dark place shining the light of the Lord and it was not going to always be acceptable. I also knew that I was not responsible for how God moves on a person. But I also knew I had to respect the rules and regulations of the facility. I will always respect the order of the house! But I will never stagnate the flow of the Holy Spirit, either. In every church service we had in the prisons, at least 20 to 30 men were giving their lives to Christ. One particular Sunday, that same man who had levitated a few Sundays ago, walked up to me to thank me. He went on to tell me that I did not know it at the time, but he was the leader of a well-known gang in the prisons, and he had brought many men into his gang, and he had lots of followers. He stated that when I laid my hands on him his life did a major shift; he said he had not been the same and he knows God called him to preach.

This young man told me that now he is witnessing Jesus Christ and bringing other gang members to the Lord and to the church. He thanked me and told me to never stop allowing God to use me because he would never be the same. I remember the power of God being so strong in that place that after the services all the men gathered around me, and with my team, they started praying.

I was huddled up in the middle of a huge circle as these mighty men of God prayed and interceded. It was a phenomenal feeling; an experience I will never forget. God moved in so many ways that it's difficult to document them all because that's how awesome He is. I recall ministering one Sunday with Pastor Carl . It was just the two of us at WCI and the service at WCI was another success with men getting delivered and set free. On the way home, as we were driving down the highway, I looked out of the window and there was a white dove flying next to the car; it seemed to be flying so low but flying in sync with each motion of the vehicle.

Pastor Carl and I both knew God was letting us know that He was with us guiding us the whole time. It was simply beautiful. There is another experience that I will never erase from my memory and that was at Ohio State Penn (OSP). I was scheduled to go preach one Saturday morning and, in my mind, it was going to be like every other service: I was going to be up on the pulpit or sitting over to the side while the men sat in their seats waiting for a word from the Lord. So, I prepared my mind and my word for OSP. I had taken just one person with me because the rule of thumb was to always go with at least two people. This was to ensure that the person who was preaching would always an assistant and have someone to pray for them and drive.

In some cases, I have traveled alone into the prisons, but I really tried to keep this rule in the forefront. Anyway, as we went into OSP, we noticed that the check-in was much different than the other prisons. At the other prisons, you check in on the inside of the building; at OSP you check in on the outside of the building first, and then you check in once you enter the building. Ohio State Penn was huge, and it had at least four floors. It was as high as I could see.

The strange thing about this building was that it had no windows. It did not dawn on me at the time that with this being a super maximum-security prison it would not have windows. I had a one-track mind and that was to deliver the word. As we entered the building, I had this big knot in my stomach. I thought it was nerves but as we continued to walk through the building, and then getting on the elevator to the second floor this place looked like something off of a bad prison show. This place was like lock up itself.

As we entered the station where the guards were, I noticed handcuffs suspending from the ceiling of the walkways. As I looked down the hallways into the pods from the security guards' station, I could see cell after cell, row after row, lined up. The floors were made of bars so I could see the guards walking back and forth. For the first time, my stomach was turning, all the guards were built like The Rock, wearing black gloves, they looked like they were ready for a battle and my thoughts were, "Where am I Lord? What is this?? We met the chaplain, who was a very nice man. He gave us the run down as he walked us to this small room that we were supposed to have service in. It was a small room with six cages, a big yellow line that divided the room and three chairs on the other side of the cages.

The chaplain then informed me that it would only be about six men that would be allowed out at one time, and they would be escorted by their personal guards and placed in the cages that stood before me. My mission was to preach or teach to these men face to face while they were shackled in cages, and I was not to cross or go near this yellow line. As my stomach turned, I was anxious and curious how God was going to pull this one off. After all, I had prepared a message as usual, but this was not a usual circumstance. The guards brought the men in one by one ahead of time; and so, when we entered the room, they were shackled and standing in their cages like a bunch of animals.

Man, you talk about hard core; this was hard core prison preaching; no music and no Amens. It was quiet, and the only voices you heard was the chaplain introducing me, and then I had the floor. With my knees knocking and my teeth chattering inwardly I began to speak to these men like they were men. I looked past the tall black metal cages, and I saw the brokenness, the hurt and the fears. I laid my sermon papers down and closed my bible and spoke from the heart. I preached Jesus Christ crucified, the good news of the Gospel. When the Lord was finished, these men were crying and gave their lives over to the Lord. The chaplain was in tears and God showed up and showed out, again. After service was over, I had a chance to speak with these men. A few told me they had been locked up more than 15 years and because there are no windows, they have not seen the light of day; they had not seen the sun or breathed in the fresh air. These were the men that you hear about who stayed locked up all day and they only got to come out in the pods for only 1 hour a day. They eat, sleep and have a toilet in the cell.

My thoughts were how horrible; but I also knew that to be in a place like this, you would've had to have done some really horrible things to be locked away to this degree. I had empathy for them; but I also respected how safe the prison kept us. I also knew that some probably had not seen a woman in a while, but I did not focus on that. My focus was evangelizing the Word of God and saving souls. This experience changed my whole perspective on prison ministry and how I saw the men. My compassion grew deeper, and my mission was clear: to go set the captives free! Not physically, of course, but mentally, emotionally, and spiritually.

I had been commissioned to break yokes, the chains of bondage that had been placed around the men and women who were incarcerated. Seeing those men in cages sealed the deal! After I saw these men shackled and in cages, the fire I already had was ignited and burned within me even more. After we left the big house, we went over to the camp that was directly across the yard. It was much smaller, and it reminded me of other prison camps. This place was like a rehab center for men who dealt with drug addiction and some minor violations that did not warrant a long prison stay. This camp had a few programs, but not much, so we went in already charged and fired up from being in the big house.

We ministered Jesus Christ and told our testimonies. The men were so moved from the teaching and preaching, and how the word of God pricked their hearts, that 10 men gave their lives to Jesus Christ that day. NCCI was another place where God moved mightily. I was not only called to preach Sunday services, but I was always called upon to do conferences and revivals in the prisons.

I remember at NCCI we were invited to a conference they were having; you see, there were times where the team and I traveled and most of those times meant an overnight stay at a local hotel just so we could minister effectively and with excellence without rushing up and down the highway all the time. At this particular service I was preaching at, during the altar call, the Holy Spirit fell upon me, and I began prophesying to the men. A man walked up to me and wanted prayer, as I prayed for him, I began to speak into his life by the leading of the Holy Spirit, when all of a sudden, this man fell out in the Spirit of God and was shaking violently, balled up in the fetal position.

I knew that God was doing a metamorphosis; he was doing a quick work in and on him! I continued to pray for others, and as I looked up, I was surrounded by nothing but inmates wanting to be free. Some people would look at it as being dangerous but to be honest I had never felt so safe. During my journey in the prisons, I can say I have never been disrespected or humiliated by the inmates. When God moves, he moves, and I can truly say they saw the beauty of the Lord. As I continued to pray, I looked up and men were lying all over the floor. Some were weeping, others were worshipping, and I had those faithful men who stood at arms, watching over me and the team while praying. This was such an indescribable feeling watching the presence of God sweep through the building like a mighty rushing wind. It was incredible to experience and watch. I can honestly say that those men at NCCI were never the same and neither was I.

When God moved at NCCI, we were invited back many times. You see, some of the men who had been in The Family is First Project in WCI had transferred to NCCI, so they knew me and the passion I had to see men incarcerated set free. I want to thank those at NCCI for opening up that magnificent door of opportunity to witness Jesus Christ. There was another time we were at NCCI hosting a three-day revival. I know it sounds strange, but God had me doing some out-of-the-box stuff, and he was doing a quick work. The first day Pastor Chris preached, and it was awesome. We prayed, and people got healed and set free.

The second day his wife, Apostle Chantell, preached and this particular day we were out in the yard on a big platform with the loudspeakers. We had Minister Katina take us into worship; Loretta was there to help pray and open up the service. I remember at one point the men were dancing in the yard and praising God with us to the song, "Hold On A Change Is About To Come", and for a split second, we all forgot that were surrounded by razor wire in a security prison. At that moment, the inmates became men, and not just men, they became men of God. It was absolutely awesome.

After we danced, we entered into worship. The Holy Spirit swept through that compound, again, and this time the yard that was packed with inmates was now packed with men with their arms raised high, worshipping The Most High God. It was beautiful! More than 50 men gave their lives to Christ that day. The third day of the revival was just as powerful: just when you think God has out done Himself, he turns around and does some more.

After I preached, there were so many men that needed prayer, that I never looked at the number; I just moved, and I did not stop until everyone got what they needed from God. I was surrounded by men with their arms and hands raised up high expecting God to move, and he did. NCCI had many programs that the men were involved in. One of them was Toastmasters which was spearheaded by an inmate who used to help me at WCI. Brother Patrick S was a wiz when it came to gathering inmates together; especially, the long-term offenders. You see, most of the men that were in my program and came to the services were those doing life, but these men always held on to hope and they never gave up on educating themselves to become better men.

It always amazed me of the drive these men had and how receptive they were when it came to the teachings and church services I conducted. The crazy part that I never got past was why the church on the outside did not have this same fire! By that's another book. Most of the time the church on the outside was filled with people who wanted a good word, but you had to pull and tug them to worship; you had to jump though many hoops to get them to pray, and my God, to get them to study the word was worse than pulling teeth. So, to come into an atmosphere where your gift is wanted, accepted, and appreciated, plus they were hungry this, was like being at the well that never ran dry! I used to tell the church on the outside that everyone should go into the prison and have at least one service because it will change your whole life and give you a new perspective on God.

To really see the hunger and thirst for God was so rewarding and rejuvenating to my spirit and soul. I recall being asked to come and speak at a Toastmasters event. When I could not travel and take the whole team, I had my faithful assistant, Loretta, attend with me. At this particular event, the room was packed, and I had a chance to minister in another way. This was an opportunity to speak to them as men using the Word of God by empowering them as fathers, brothers, and sons. At the end of my speech, I was awarded a Certificate of Appreciation, which they all signed. I appreciate the opportunity to pour into such great vessels. To this day, I am a member of NCCI's Toastmasters and I'm proud of it! Another event that I was invited to host was a leadership training, and I'm telling you, NCCI was on fire. They could not get enough.

God was doing a quick work. The leadership training was called, *Reclaiming Your Identity; There Is A King In You,* and was hosted by Power and Praise Production, which was spearheaded by Brother Patrick K, another inmate with an awesome call on his life. I would like to thank him for all his hard work and efforts as well. This men's retreat packed the house with over 100 men in one room. I remember the gym room being huge, filled with tables, and each table seated 10 to 12 men. They did not care if they were smashed next to each other; they wanted a word from God. I also recall that when the tables were full, they pulled out extra chairs; and when they could not place any more chairs, men were standing along the walls.

I taught on identity and characteristics of a king, and leadership. I could tell that the chaplain who was standing in the back was not pleased with what I was saying nor did he like the fact that I could fill the room with so many men when he struggled to get 10 men to his services on a Sunday. This is not speculation or an observation; this is facts, this is what he told me, himself. You see, some of the men who held high positions in the prisons never failed to remind me that I was woman and the only reason so many men came to the services was just to look at me. This is when my tough skin had to be activated, then I had to remind them of the anointing that destroys the yoke, and not Stacie, so I kept it moving.

Nevertheless, during the men's retreat the men asked questions and took notes. It was an all-day event and very blessed. At the end, I prayed for some men, but there were five men who the Lord told me to establish in their offices as Apostle, Prophet, Evangelist, Pastor and Teacher. They had these calls on their lives and had been working hard for some years. So, I obeyed the Holy Spirit and anointed them and laid my hands on their bellies, imparting that supernatural anointing and establishing them. As we were leaving, riding in the cart back to the main building, the chaplain said to Loretta and me, "Now, they think their somebody", referring to the inmates. He said, "You have to be careful not to encourage them too much or they will walk around like they have power." We did not even respond to what he was saying. I knew that a spirit of jealousy and envy had entered in him, and I was not about to entertain that spirit. When Loretta and I got into the car, she looked at me and said, "Apostle, He did not like all that you did today.

You showed him up and from what he said when we were on our way back to the main building, I feel he is going to do something to shut you down." I did not dwell on it much; we prayed and kept it moving. I want to give a special shout out to the volunteer coordinator Mrs. Steward; she was another strong black woman who paved the way for may programs and she believed that people could and would change. I know, and witnessed, her long lasting faith and commitment. So, thank you Mrs. S for running with my vision and opening up the door!

We continued to minster at WCI, LOCI and many other prisons where the Spirit of God was showing up and doing mighty things. By this time, I had followed the instructions of the Holy Spirit and launched The Family is First Project into other prisons; so now, instead of just being at WCI, we were at LOCI and NCCI. I was feeling pretty good, and living my dream, walking in prophetic purpose that I had worked so many years for. This was a lot of work being in three different prisons, but I was up for the job. You see, each man represented a family of more than two members, so, at WCI, I had 25 men, at LOCI, I had 27 men and at NCCI, I had 40 men. To help us with the teaching, I had alumni which were inmates that had graduated from the program and were trained by me and skilled to help me facilitate the class when I could not be there. I was confident in what I was doing, and with all the materials that I accumulated over the years, and once pieced together, I had a full-blown teaching course. With that, I developed my books, wrote my proposals, and developed my purchase orders because, I knew I could no longer continue to volunteer and give my materials away operating on two shoestrings and a straw.

One of the hardest parts about ministry is the finances. I had leaders teach me about being a servant, but they failed to tell me the importance about people sowing into your vision. You see, materials, traveling and hosting people all accumulate a cost, and it was coming out of my pocket for years. I was on my 10th year and determined to shift my program and my mindset and do something different. So, I typed up my purchase order and submitted it to the prisons, and they accepted my terms. It felt good to finally be compensated for all my hard work; but the money was more for the price of the books, to take care of my team expenses and travel. I knew deep down that I was building on shaky ground being a strong Black woman, walking in my Apostolic calling. I knew that I was in a man's world, but I was bulldozing my way through. For 10 years, The Family is First Project was going strong.

The prisons had even agreed to allow me to Jpay (inmate email) my facilitators which were the men who were helping me teach the class. I was fully connected and, on a roll; or so I thought. I was even approached by the federal prisons in Ohio. I passed their security check and was awaiting an orientation date. My dream was to take The Family is First Project nationwide and I was headed that way. I was walking in the prophetic promises that had been spoken over my life, time and time again. I am so thankful today because I got an opportunity to see the fruit of all my labor and hard work.

It reminds me of the scripture, *1 Corinthians 3:6-9 I have planted, Apollos watered; but God gave the increase. So then neither is he that planteth anything, neither he that watereth; but God that giveth the increase. Now he that planteth and he that watereth are one: and every man shall receive his own reward according to his own labour (KJV).*

Reading these scriptures reminds me that when you are planting and watering … it is not an easy process; when you are working for the Lord, exercising your gifting and allowing Him to flow through you, you don't really think about all the pressures and pains. It really does not hit home, all the work you put in, until you have completed that phase of your life. That is when you see how God increased what he placed in your hands, as you were moving all along.

A PICTURE SPEAKS MORE THAN A THOUSAND WORDS!

THE REVIVAL

THE REVIVAL PART 2

Ephesians 4:11-16 *And he gave some, apostles; and some, prophets; and some, evangelists; and some, pastors and teachers; For the perfecting of the saints, for the work of the ministry, for the edifying of the body of Christ: Till we all come in the unity of the faith, and of the knowledge of the Son of God, unto a perfect man, unto the measure of the stature of the fulness of Christ:*

SPOKEN WORD

(Untitled)

I want to thank Apostle Stacie Johnson who taught me a lot of things but most of all for teaching me to not allow those people who won't except change, I have to change my perception of those people and the situation, so it does not affect me. Raised in unstable households but we really never had a choice, if there was times we needed to feel loved and just communicate, but we rarely had a voice. As infants we were taught and encouraged to speak, but as kids when even something important to say why were we often forced to listen. So when no one wanted to hear us, we acted out for more attention. Yet the attention we get was not the attention we wanted, because the attention you usually gave was distant, which should have been a conversation or two of finding out what's wrong with your children. With that alone being deprived from equality of equal opportunity, most are surrounded by poverty and drug infested violence that surround the community, so tell me, what could you have expected this to be of me? Because seed planted in bad soil, knowing our history how could you of not known the results, Where we were born and raised destiny's projects, were just a manifestation of their thoughts. In this place, it was just a project that projected into a profit of course strictly for the government. And yet they want us to think it was all coincidental as if we would not tell that it was all orchestrated, beautifully like an instrumental. Designed to keep us away from them and at war with each other killing our own, friends and family which didn't matter to them as long as they were our own color. Yet they say black lives matter but really to who? We have been killing our own for dedicates without a problem they have too. You see I find it ironic in saying that everything that was once a disgrace to our race we now embrace, killings in our homes down to the disrespect we show our mothers, to the derogatory language we use toward one another, Snitching is at an all-time high which is often done out of fear of losing a lover and loyalty is no longer honor its often challenged by a cover. They say silence is golden and in the streets that's true, but I beg to differ when it comes to parents raising their youth. By Donald

"If you want to change attitudes, start with a change in behavior." Quote by -William Glasser.

CHAPTER SEVEN

FROM BOYS TO MEN

I REMEMBER LIKE IT was yesterday. In addition to the Family is First project, I started teaching out of Dr. Tony Evans; book, Kingdom Man. This particular class was for my alumni who needed that extra leadership training. It did not take them long to adapt to the concept of becoming a kingdom man. They had already been through the process of change and transition in their minds. They had been reconciled with their families, and now they needed that extra push towards leadership. This meant that I had to now trust and allow them to facilitate the Family is First Project without my help. In some classes, I was only present to observe them because I knew that they were fully equipped, locked, and loaded, and ready to facilitate certain lessons.

I did not know it then, but God blessed me with one of the biggest men's ministries in prison that a woman has ever had. I was the first Black woman to go behind bars to have a program that not only taught and trained men but also facilitated healing and reconciliation to the families. Through my passion and deepest desires, the Lord allowed me to pave the way for those programs and ministries who would come after me. I did not realize the magnitude of what I was doing then because I was in the thick of it all; but now I see what God was doing. As he was developing them, he was developing and positioning me for something greater! I like the way Dr Tony Evans puts it when addressing the men. He says, ***"If we, as men, could ever fully comprehend all that God has not only intended for us but has also provided for us, we would not only improve our own lives, as well as our families', but we would also impact our churches, communities, and the entire world."***(*Kingdom Man, Dr. Tony Evans*).

When The Family is First Project first started, I used to look out at my audience, and all I saw was a bunch of boys who committed crimes and were locked up trying to survive. They had broken homes and relationships; they were selfish, prideful and some, were very arrogant. I watched these boys play on women's hearts and string them along just to get a food or clothes box, and most of all, I watched them manipulate women to get money placed on their books. I watched many relationships crumble due to lack of purpose and vision in God. These families just did not know how to talk and communicate with one another.

I was placed in rooms with violent angry boys who had trust issues and did not how to control their feelings; boys who suffered from addictions and insecurity. I was with boys who were unsure about my motives, at first, and some did not know what to expect when they entered the program. But when these boys began to grow up and grasp who they were and what their real roles were in God, they became MEN! They became men of valor and men of purpose; they became men who could lead their families regardless of their demographic location. They became responsible individuals over their finances, and they learned how to control their emotions and communicate their real feelings. They became living walkers of God's word. These men tapped into their true gifts and started launching into other areas within the prison system shining their lights in dark places.

These Real Men built upon the foundation that was laid by the Family Is First Project and they took what they learned and applied it to their daily lives. They became THE SONS OF THURNDER, the Real Men behind bars. These men gained a newfound respect for their women, and they were willing to release all the bad habits and foolishness that had entangled them for many of their prison years. These boys allowed me to walk them through their processes of healing, deliverance, and growth until they tapped into their Manhood, their Kingdom Manhood. Thank God for his Holy Spirit who moved through me to touch these men's lives for lasting change and put them on the road for true headship.

The primary principle upon which your destiny forms as a Kingdom man, both now and in the future, involves the concept of headship—alignment. How is your alignment when it comes to authority, dominion, and courageous ruling? Who do you submit to? How does that show? (DR. Tony Evans)

1 Corinthians 13:11-13 *When I was a child, I spake as a child, I understood as a child, I thought as a child: but when I became a man, I put away childish things.*

CHAPTER EIGHT

SISTA SOLDIERS

A S THE FAMILY IS FIRST PROJECT was well on the rise, and the ministry, Adonai Ministries name was ringing in the prisons. I was called upon to come to the women's prison. As much as I enjoyed worshipping in the men's prison, I must say that there is nothing like being in a room full of broken women who have lost everything and nothing to lose. These women were ready and willing for their healing. I remember their excitement every time I came. They were amazed to see a strong black beautiful woman full of the Holy Spirit preach as hard as a man but yet remain soft and virtuous.

I remember so many times the power of God falling in that place and women lying all over the floor as God was working on them. Looking back there were so many women who had calls on their lives and they were determined to press in and get all that they needed from God. Some of these women had been so beaten down and battered in the world that prison became their safe haven, their place of true transformation. I remember in one of the services one of the ladies gave her testimony of how grimy she was when she first entered the prison world. She spoke of how she manipulated and abused other women so she could survive, and how she was constantly sent to the "hole" for her behavior.

This particular inmate did not mind sharing openly about how she was so hurt over the circumstances of how she got incarcerated; but, she said when I preached and prophesied to her it was like an angel coming to confirm what God told her in her cell. That day she received a touch from God, and she said her life would never be the same. There were so many women who were so giving, and ready to receive, that still today, I consider them my daughters in the Lord. I was always well received with love at DCI and Marysville and the power and anointing of God shall always rest on those places because of the labor of love and road which has already been plowed.

Not to mention, they had and still have some very good chaplains who really care about their spiritual lives and desire to see them grow. Having a church service in the women's prison was fairly easy because we were welcomed in with open arms. The struggle came in when I tried to place the Family is First Project there. You see, The Family is First Project was designed to reconnect the inmates with their families.

The sad thing is that the women who are incarcerated don't get many family visits and the families were not eager to come into the prisons and sit with them. This was very disturbing because in the men's prison the women and mothers flock to support the men. The visiting rooms were always packed out and these women did not mind spending their time and money to make sure the men had what they needed. But when it came to the women who were locked up, they barely got visits. I remember one Saturday morning I had an engagement at the prison, and for those who don't know, Saturdays are very busy in the visitation room; especially, in the men's prison. But when I walked past the visitation room in the women's prison, I was shocked to see only a few people sitting. This was very upsetting to me because I knew from my own experiences of having a husband incarcerated, how important it was that family supported and visited. I was curious as to why it was so different for the women, so I went straight to the source! The Family is First Project was very difficult to get into the women's prison, and it was not because of any red tape with the prison, it was the lack of participation with the families. Believe me, I tried.

I reached out and called them. Some were on board and others were just not interested. So, I focused on the women, and I deigned the program to fit their needs. I held a small group session with about 10 women: some of them would be returning home while others were doing more than 10 years. Sitting in those group sessions, I learned so much from those ladies. For example, they told us that they only get three pairs of underwear a month and if they came on their monthly cycle, they had to hand wash them out and wear the stained ones until their month was up.

These women went on to tell us that because of the lack of support, they don't get much commissary, so they had to do things that went against their morals and values just to have the basic things, like hygiene. I saw the sadness in their eyes as I talked with them. There was an emptiness that I had never seen with the men in my time of teaching and facilitating groups. This emptiness was a deep-down hurt that stemmed from being rejected by those family members and others who promised to be there, but never showed up. This was a pain of being left for dead in a dark place that barely had any light. A place that was so corrupt, some did not have a choice in adapting to the ways of prison life to survive. Listening to them with empathy gave to a great compassion and understanding why God needed soldiers to go in the dark and set the captives free. Keep in mind that it was not mine to judge, whether or not if their stories were true. I was there on a mission and to be that listening hear, coming to preach hope, healing, and deliverance.

I understood why their worship was real and their praise was non-negotiable. I understood why they flocked to the Sunday services and desired to get all the God they could. I could clearly see the passion and desire they had to be free, not just free physically, but mentally, emotionally, and spiritually. These women are the true sista soldiers. They pressed past their pain; they turned their misery into their ministry; and in spite of the odds against them, they continued to love God with a deep belief that whatever they experienced they were going to survive! So, every time we came, the sanctuary was packed with women's arms and hands raised, ready to receive. I want to personally thank them all for the love and support and for holding my arms up but most of all for having a ready spirit to glean and absorb all that God had for them through His Word and the laying on of hands. Let your voices be heard and continue to speak your truth!

Proverbs 31:25 She is clothed with strength and dignity, and she laughs without fear of the future.

THE VOICES OF THE SISTA SOILDERS

Unafraid unbothered carried by God and in an instant your life can change for the good or for the bad. On one sunny day a grown man pulled a gun on me and my son, the boys mother addressed the situation and thought that everything was squashed taken care of. I did not know I would be doing 11 years in prison because of this, away from my four children along with a grandbaby that was just born. You are talking upside down and right side up; my children are my world I will give my last breath for them. they went through a storm not wanting to live with anybody, I was left wondering if someone is bothering my children, I couldn't protect them laying on a steel bed being told when to take a shower and to line up to eat, that wasn't my future for me and my children.

After 5 years of incarceration my oldest son was murdered, I went in a very dark place not wanting to bathe, eat, drink, talk or listen to anyone not even God. I had told myself I have a lot of questions for God, I'm trying to figure out why my son? I was already away from my son, he was holding me down making my kids do what they needed to do, and he was a kid itself, again my life was turned upside down. I was embarrassed at the fact I have four children facing obstacles trials and tribulations alone and only wanting their mothers love and attention. So, that brought me down even more, after 5 months I start talking to God and he answered me and God told me I would never leave you nor forsake you, I was always here just waiting on you.

At that moment I literally dropped to my knees, at the chapel the most caring chaplain I've ever met when the devil thought that he took me with my son the chaplain told me one word, you won! I didn't understand it for a second, I went back and laid down and I thought about it. When you make your first step to do something different and change in a positive way, that means you won, and from that day forward, I leaned only on God, and I never asked him another question as to why. I figured out who He was. After the first two months, moving forward I was moved to DCI correctional the atmosphere was different the energy was set for change, I knew then God was definitely in the midst of it all, my family was closer, and the staff was amazing. it was really about family.

My son's birthday came up and I was allowed to do a balloon release inside of a prison, look at God! again He was giving me comfort He was showing me it was going to be okay that I'm with you my daughter and then boom here come this woman of God (Apostle Stacie) with this amazing group, The Family is First Project allowed me to express myself on different levels of returning home giving me a light at the end of my tunnel guaranteeing me that I'm not alone in this group. we shared different topics. We had homework, we prayed together, we had emotional days together, and overall, it gave me a sense of security because today I'm still connected to this woman of God.

Apostle Stacie introduced me to her wonderful husband Apostle Frank a man of God, I'm very grateful for the support team that I have once I was released. I then felt the love from the woman of God herself and her husband and her team, they showed me that I can make it, I have the tools and it's up to me to put my best foot forward and never give up. I've been home for 5 years, I'm blessed to have 14 grandkids, 13 god kids and I'm just grateful. I'm in a good place in my life, I have a job, I have my own home, I have my own car, and most of all I have a man that sits high and looks low, and His name is Jesus! I am truly blessed on today.

With much peace,

Shannon M.

* * *

Hello, my name is LaToya #889??? is the number that will be attached to my past for the rest of my life, but it is not attached to the glory of the Most High God. I just came home March 22, 2021, after an 8-year sentence for aggravated robbery. I'm here to say those 8 years was the beginning of finding my purpose and my destiny. Prison was not easy, but God had a plan and a ministry for my life. The first couple of years was tuff because I left my 7-year-old daughter out here and I thought I was not going to make it. I felt as if I couldn't breathe without my baby, I just couldn't understand how such a loving God can take the only thing away from me, we'll at least that's what my flesh thought.

I was a quiet person scared and confused but I heard God's voice clear as day telling me I gave my only son for you so just walk through this valley and allow me to use you. I still cried and fussed, but then I said OK God. You see I was one of those people the world took advantage of, if you know what I mean. I had my innocence taken at the tender age of 7 and boy, it turned me cold as ice! But as I walked into that prison, I knew I was tired, and I no longer wanted that anger anymore, so I knew through this new journey I had to allow God to use me properly. I became a part of the praise ministry and became a praise dancer for the prison, every week a new ministry came in to spread Gods word but this particular month a new ministry walked in Adonai Ministries, and when I say they came in, you felt nothing but the Holy Ghost!

And the moment the woman of God Apostle Stacie Johnson opened her mouth I knew she was sent by the Most High, demons instantly had to bow down. She did not come to play, everything in that building seem to look different around me, I knew I was important to God but the fire on the inside of Apostle Stacie was almost like when Elizabeth seen Mary and the babies jumped, that's how my spirit felt every time she came, she did not give up on us, she came every week to the point she started a group The Family Is First Project!

And omg, it impacted the lives of us women to the point I was thirsty for more of the word and it was a blessing to know that it was really someone praying for us. When her ministry no longer came, I felt as if a piece of my soul was snatched, you see the enemy was so scared of the power of God to the point the guards were even being delivered when Adonai Ministries came through, they came through with such anointing and purpose you knew they were sent by God himself! Today I have reconnected with my spiritual mom Apostle Stacie on the outside, and I have joined her ministry as she continues to set the captives free!

With Love,

LaToya T

POEM

Why I Thank You

To get to my truths there was always a twist and sometimes a turn and after that was a sign that said do not disturb.

I really wasn't open to doing anything but this prison time and not letting the time do me.

Then I was introduced to Stacie Johnson and she showed me what I refused to see, you know how it is, you're like the family is first project another certificate. But then, I was like the family is first? That's when I got interested.

I still wasn't digging deep cause I felt like an outsider, until I became honest with myself and started to write I'm a liar.

My mind started to open to things I use to reject, my heart started to love things I couldn't accept.

I'm not letting my past define me, I know I've been led astray, and me applying myself to the family is first project has shown me the way.

I've set short term goals and long-term goals and learned to activity listen; I'm taking things like that with me forward so I can be in the right position.

So, Apostle Stacie please believe that its important the things you do, and your roadies Katina, Tonya, and Loretta, thank you too!

By Z

CHAPTER NINE

WCI —THE VOICES

FIRST AND FOREMOST, I would like to thank God for everything He has put me through because it is He who made me what I am today. I want to thank the families for all your time, love, support, and commitment. You all have the faith to keep us going, even through the worst circumstances. It took a while to adjust and be vocal in the beginning, but I had to ask myself why did I sign up for The Family Is First Project if I'm not going to interact and involve myself within the program? So, then I challenged myself to trust Apostle Stacie and accept what God gave her to give me and I have not turned back since.

My greatest accomplishment from this program was it taught me my role and purpose as a man and my role within my family. Apostle Stacie, as a woman, exposed me to why God created man and the purpose God has for me as a man. You see, at first, I thought a man was only supposed to be a provider financially for his family and that a man did not hit females, but a man had a lot of females. But that picture I painted was wrong; Apostle Stacie and her alumni team taught me a different point of view: A man is supposed to be a provider, but also a protector, a cultivator, a teacher, and a leader. A Man is required by God to fulfill all those things which is his true reason for creating man. Knowing that, I now have accepted God's challenge for His purpose in my life. To discover my purpose, I had to get a vision, and then I asked myself, what is a vision? A vision means to see something come into view as if it were already there. I had to think past being incarcerated and use this time as preparation time instead of jail time so I could accomplish my vision until being incarcerated came to an end. I began to put into practice my time management skills and improve in my decision making.

Doing so has allowed me to be better at pursuing God's true purpose that he has for me. I learned that not every purpose is known to us because we have to understand God's original intent for us. This program has brought me closer with the Lord. I now attend service and pray daily. I read His word and I practice His way of living. Now I have the understanding I once lacked, and I'm living. I plan on living the remainder of my life through God's original intent instead of the intent of my own or my friends. Apostle Stacie challenged me to reach within myself and pull out my fullest potential.

I now see what she saw in me! Apostle Stacie, this is what I give to you: thank you for everything you taught me. I truly want you to know that you are amazing. You are an exceptional woman of God; you are an excellent role model for many men and women, including myself. You are one of the most impactful people in my life. And it is you who helped me to take a turn in my life for the better; it is you who taught me all the skills to be a leader not only for my family but also the people outside of my family circle. It is you who bonded me and my girl closer together and helped us both adapt to a prison relationship. You are one of the most loving, caring, inspirational, passionate, strong, brave, graceful, unselfish person that I've ever met. And you are a woman above all women which makes my respect for you shoot past the moon! You are wonderful and I hope you get a chance to spread this program into other prisons. I have been praying for you and I thank you one last time. Remember, it's not over!

With a pure heart,

Patterson

***

The Family Is First Project showed me how to help my loved ones without becoming a burden on them. My mother understood certain things about how prison worked but The Family Is First Project gave her shining insight that not only kept me focused, but it made me want to strive for greater things while I was in prison to help change my life so that when I am released from this world of bondage and placed back into the world of liberty I can strive towards greater goals...Thank you very much for reaching out to me and letting my story be shared.

With love and respect Diahntae

The journey through The Family is First Project was the best experience I have experienced during incarceration. The Family First Project helped me with identifying leadership, faith, hope, and joy due to the circumstances I faced and being able to have a healthy relationship with family and friends which has made my time and bond positive, strong and reliable. The Family Is First Project helped my family and friends cope with my time better and have faith and joy walking this journey along with me and gave them insight on how to ride through the journey mentally and physically.

The Family Is First Project touched family members and made it easier to consider visiting and supporting their loved ones and see they were trying to change and better themselves regardless the circumstances. When I first started The Family Is First Project, I was shy like a turtle, and as time went by, I came out of my shell and my purpose and my leadership in life was exposed to me. I learned how to speak in front of groups and how much influence I had on others and touched them with my words and hope knowing I was sentenced to double life; but, I kept a smile on my face and always put out positive and powerful energy. I always found a way to find good out of a bad situation and make light. I didn't just go through trials and tribulations, I grew through them and that's what helped me be the person I am today, even though I still fall short sometimes.

But I know my plan and purpose in life and The Family Is First Project gave me that vision and I will never forget or stop applying what I learned from The Family Is First Project. The Family Is First Project and thanks for giving me that opportunity to learn and grow. Believing and having hope and staying positive has given me a second chance at life. Now I have an out date and blessed to still be strong and healthy due to this crisis we face. Peace and blessing to all my Family Is First Project family and friends...

Forever blessed, Eric

***

When I first began the Family is First Project, I really didn't know what to expect, but upon my first meeting I felt that this class could help me change the way I looked at things, and the fact that Apostle Stacie Johnson would not be having no nonsense in her presence. We quickly found out that these powerful and strong ladies of the Family is First Project were very relatable. I quickly took to the class and the lessons that it was instilling in me. You know, sometimes when your locked up, you can easily lose focus on the morals of life and get caught up in the facade of prison. Understanding and being a man and leader to your woman and kids is the reality of life but you can easily get away from this being locked up and from what really matters to your family and the example you set for them.

Being attentive when your woman or kids is having a bad day; being a good listener and then giving good advice; knowing that what you say matters as the head of the family, even locked up, or not being the financial support you once were, I learned that you are still a valuable an irreplaceable factor to the household emotionally, spiritually, psychologically, and mentally. You can still be the rock and glue that keeps the family going. That's what The Family Is First Project helped me realize: that I am still an asset to my family. I learned how to understand my new role and how to motivate my loved ones daily. These are the type of things that this class taught me. It became instinct to become a problem solver, counselor, and nurturer. It taught me how to make sure me and my family is on the same page. The Family Is First Project did that for me. It made me a better leader, father, husband, and man.

A man of understanding; a man of resolve. An alpha by nature, a nurturer by habit. These traits are ones that many of us have in us already. To cement these traits into your routine, daily, will take work and practice; but, with a program like this, that goal was easily achievable. This powerful woman that ran this program is a God-send, and given the opportunity, anyone and everyone should experience it. It helped me with myself, and my everyday life with my family and kids. I want to thank everyone that played a part in The Family is First Project and my growth, and I want to thank you, Apostle Stacie, for letting me share my story.

Thank you and God bless,

Ronald

***

The Family Is First Project changed my life tremendously. As a result of going through this program, and becoming a facilitator, I became impactful. I'm able to lead with great boldness. I still carry those tools that was given to me. I discovered my role as a man. It's very rare to be able to operate in his or her gift- while being incarcerated. However, this program offered a platform that allowed me, and many others, to operate in their full potential. My family felt the love in the room, in every family meeting. That alone helped me and my family get through a stressful time. This program covered real life issues and addressed them. I truly believe this program added value to all the participants.

A typical visit in prison could be stressful. It's next to impossible to discuss real issues on a regular visit. In my opinion, it's too many distractions, too much stress, and not enough time. This program produced a learning environment. I was able to process different information and help make good decisions. I was in my early twenties, and I was able to block out anything that was unproductive. I was very fortunate to not join the gang or become an antagonist or getting involved with drugs. I wanted to be better for my family and live out what we believe in. I believe in putting my family first. I represent my family, even now. I will never forget being behind a panel, in a prison visitation room, answering questions.

I was able to share my thoughts around my family, who never seen me move in that fashion. It was a sight to see. I actually grew up in prison. I was a teenager when I first started this journey. Before prison I was in the streets. I sold drugs in a high crime area. I couldn't see another way.

My goal was becoming rich by selling drugs. I have a great family that really loves me. I graduated high school and went on to college. However, I had one foot in the streets. This program helped me take that one foot out of the streets... Now, I'm walking this thing out! A lot of people that know my story always say I have a lot of peace, even while being in prison for a murder I didn't do. I always say, "Moving in my gift gives me peace." This program changed the trajectory of my life. I was able to relate to Apostle Stacie Johnson, who is my Spiritual Mother. Apostle Stacie Johnson has imparted strength, hope, and value inside me. I am what's considered a model inmate.

I have a perfect institutional record. I have done many great things, even while being in prison. I'm a 3rd class stationary steam engineer. This license allows me to operate in any plant in the state of Ohio. I learned that a boiler is a closed metal container in which water is heated to produce steam. Steam is the vapor that forms when water is heated to its boiling point, that is 212°F. Before being involved in The Family Is First Project, I was like a vessel, just holding water. I wasn't even considering producing anything.

That water I was holding was equal to, but not limited to: Gifts, talents, ideas, and visions. I was just holding water. I was on standby. This Family Is First Project came with fire (a new flame). That fire turned my water into steam and put me online. What was inside me began to be released. I was able to produce. I'm forever grateful to be a part of greatness. Now, I carry that fire. I pray that both Apostle Frank and Apostle Stacie be blessed in all they do.

Thank You!!
Charles (CW)

***

The Family Is First Project helped change my life in a big way. Before being in The Family Is First Project, I was going to the hole about two times a month for fighting, disrespect or being out of place. But my first day in The Family Is First Project, Apostle Stacie Johnson told the group "You define yourselves by your own decisions" and "Don't make decisions off of what other people think about you." I knew then God had a purpose for me to be in this class. Once Apostle Stacie said those words, I went back to the block and locked myself down and asked myself some serious questions: am I living the life I want to live? or am I living the life to impress other people?

The things that I was doing weren't making me or my family happy. The stuff I was doing was only making the people who I thought were my family, happy. I had to relook at my life and understand why the people I call my friends only cheer for me when I do something wrong. And why the people I thought were my friends wasn't with me when I got locked up, shot or even when my mama's house got shot up. So, me being in The Family Is First Project helped me to understand I don't live my life off other people's thoughts. The Family Is First Project gave me a lot of information and tools I need for life, not only in prison but when I return home. The Family Is First Project helped me to know if I don't have a solid plan, then I plan to fail. This helped me to get rid of the criminal mindset by getting rid of old patterns and habits.

It helped me to understand how to deal with my feelings and my family relationships. I feel if a lot of today's youth know the information that The Family Is First Project has to give, it can help them stop coming to prison and stop thinking that the streets is the only way they have a life. Because now I know my life has more purpose and I know I went through my struggles so I can help other young people with their struggles. Now I don't have any hatred in my heart anymore, so I thank God for using Apostle Stacie Johnson to help me change my mindset and my family situation. So, I pray many blessings over Apostle Stacie Johnson and the Family Is First Project.

Genuwine

***

The Family Is First Project has been very beneficial and eye-opening to myself and many others. We focused on many of the key elements that are necessary to make relationships successful both during the time while we were incarcerated and because, especially, when we returned home. Keys, such as recognizing barriers and relationships, establishing healthy boundaries, identifying triggers that lead to anger, effective time management, and budgeting, just to name a few, and it doesn't stop there. In the alumni class we go even deeper as we discussed and studied many components of leadership. We discovered the realm of influence we each have and the importance of being a man of integrity as we lead not only our families but also many others in our communities, workplaces, churches, and people that we interact with. In addition to our regular assignments, Apostle Stacie had us study the book called Kingdom Man by Dr. Tony Evans.

This book really broke down the many facets of manhood from a big biblical perspective, and this is what also makes The Family Is First Project so successful because it's rooted in biblical principles. The Bible is our handbook for life and is filled with all the instructions to live a successful life. It must be the foundation upon which every kingdom man builds his life and family upon. We live in a world and a society that has strayed so far away from the biblical principles that families were once built upon and it's not surprising to see the breakdown of the family unit that is so common today.

As kingdom men we are called to be different, to stand boldly on the word of God and to be leaders of this generation. But this must begin by all of us having a personal relationship with our heavenly father before we can be successful in our own personal relationships. God must be the head of our lives before we can be the head of our families.

So, thank you Apostle Stacie Johnson, sister Loretta, and sister Katina. Some people might think it to be a little odd that we have these three women teaching us how to be kingdom men, but I can assure you that they are no-nonsense and are more capable of doing the job! Their success only further proves the need for more people to step up to the plate and fulfill their God-given calling of building disciples. Thank you all for your commitment to The Family Is First Project and to each one of us. I also want to thank each and every family member for their support and patience with us throughout our incarceration.

Ryan B

* * *

I used to get in so much trouble and I think so little of myself. To be honest, I thought of harming myself so many times. I felt like I had nobody in this world and everybody had turned their back on me. I felt like nobody loved me. Not my family, my kids, not even God. I heard about The Family Is First Project, and it was something in me that made me sign up and be a part of this movement. Apostle Stacie opened up my eyes and light to the meaning of love and trust in God. If anyone were to check my prison record, I don't get tickets. I do all programs and I passed all my drug tests.

This program found me in the lowest and darkest part of my life, and it saved me! Yes, I am a convict, and I made a lot of mistakes in my life but I'm human. I'm somebody's father, son, brother and husband. I'm worth being loved. I'm worth being forgiven. Apostle Stacie Johnson taught us all these things. She taught us how to walk and carry ourselves. She taught us how to believe and trust and love God. Without The Family Is First Project, I don't know where I would have been. I don't know how I would've learned how to fix and mend my relationship with my family. Apostle Stacie saves lives, and she saves families. So many of us that are incarcerated thank God for her. The men in prison took time to listen to her. We seen her passion, her struggles in pushing her vision and the lives she continually changes before we can get out to change the world. So much is going on in this crazy world; our kids are watching us, so, if we are to come home working, doing what kings are supposed to do, our kids will follow in the same manner and our communities would be a better place. Thank you, Apostle Stacie, for guiding me and for taking time out of your life to help all of us grow. I believe in you and The Family Is First Project if no nobody else does. God bless you and your home.

Lendale F

* * *

The Family Is First Project has been such a big help to me since I've been locked up. It has helped me to be more understanding as a man and it has helped me to develop my family relationships with my older sister, younger sister, and my oldest niece. The Family Is First Project showed me how to improve my character and become a man of integrity.

I'm proud to be the person that I am today. I know it will not be easy when I get out; life has changed, but with the help of The Family Is First Project teachings, and my family, I know I will be just fine. I want to do so many things. Today, I am a positive person. I look forward to the day when I return home. Apostle Stacie Johnson's program, The Family Is First Project has taught us so much, even how to give back to our community. When I return home, I hope to accomplish everything I need to do, and I promise myself, and God, that I will use the skills that I have learned in The Family's First Project. I know living is one day at a time and I'm willing to do what it takes to make it. I want to thank Apostle Stacie and The Family Is First Project for all that she has done for me and my family.

Haywood

* * *

The Family Is First Project is so powerful and anointed. The things the Family Is First Project did for me and my family still lives inside of us today. Apostle Stacie Johnson helped me become the man I am today, showing me the experience and true meaning of family. At the beginning, I was so broken; mad at everybody and everything, including my family, but after applying the principles from The Family Is First Project, I began to see change inside of myself and my family. Boldness came inside of me where I began to pray for my family on phone and visits. And also, they seen me live out the prayers in front of them.

One thing that sticks out to me was when Apostle Stacie used to have our families get up in front of everybody and let out all their frustration that we have built up inside of our family from being so selfish and full of ourselves. It made me really realize that I needed to work on me, and it did work. Thank you so much Apostle Stacie and the Family Is First Project. It has been in operation over a decade now, and my family is still together., Love and blessings Marty

* * *

Apostle Stacie,

I believe the greatest impact The Family Is First Project has had on me, first of all, is the example that you all displayed as a couple. The love and communication was evident. I learned that I was very selfish, and to have a God-centered relationship, I must put my spouse first. This has allowed me to really invest in her by listening and being attentive to her needs. I learned that if we keep Jesus at the center of our union it will not be based on our personal opinions but on what thus says the Lord! The greatest thing I took away with me was learning to develop and cultivate the seed that attracted Chantee' to me in the first place. That seed for me was honesty, so I make a responsibility to always be up front and honest. I also learned a lot from the other couples. I still teach on the different levels of relationship that you all taught. I praise God for your vision, continue to be obedient. Jesus loves you and so do I

Tony R.

* * *

I would like to thank all parties that had a part in The Family Is First Project. Since I've been a part of this program, I've learned tools that will help me to better myself and my family. Before I joined this program my dad and I were not on good terms; but since I've use some of the skills Apostle Stacie taught, our relationship has grown as well as other family members who I wasn't in contact with. I have an older sister who was not in my life, or her children. Now thanks to The Family Is First Project, they are all back in my life, so I cannot thank you enough for strengthening that bond. My relationship with my mom and kids has gotten that much tighter and better.

By learning active listening, they now know I'm not just hearing them I'm in tune with what they are saying and feeling. Most of all, The Family Is First Project taught me how to deal with self and put God in the driver seat. Apostle Stacie taught me how the fruit of the spirit will take you further than anything of this world and how I must walk in truth, love, and contentment and how to live my life in the light of God. So, many blessings to all who played a part in my growth and bless all the men and women who are connected to you.

Forever grateful Antron

* * *

It would take a book by itself, by me and my wife, to fully express what The Family Is First Project has done and meant to us... but with as much brevity as I can muster, I must say that The Family Is First Project revealed to me that there was a need to bring all of my relationships out of the sand and onto a rock... how to re-strengthen them and fortify them and untangle them from demonic pressure, stress and witchcraft control. It taught me personally how to un-pressurize and fix what I never even knew needed to be fixed in my own life. It taught me how to unburden the ones I love and who loved me so that they could still be free to live out their own lives as they chose to maintain their love, bond, and support for me. I learned that family was not just blood-related, but it also consists of those who, by their own volition, choose to be about you in a way that one could count on and trust to be what family ought to really be...

Loyalty, love, empathy, honesty, humanity and trust all wrapped up in a devotion that allows everyone involved to not lose themselves of their own lives as they interact with one's incarcerated life, assisting them through this jungle of a journey. As one blows the shofar to activate and anoint and cleanse and empower the atmosphere... knowing that in doing so the blower of the shofar experiences a cleansing, a purging, and an impartation of power in return. So as did I, a co- facilitator alongside Apostle Stacie while distributing wisdom, knowledge, and life coaching family fortified information...

I was renewed, regenerated, repaired, and replenished to refuel others to discover their individual ordained ordered steps that will work out their solutions and answers to their family and life situations they never even knew that they, too, truly needed. I am forever thankful, grateful, and appreciative for this connection and experience... for I believe it has added something deep and worthwhile inside of me for others to one day discover. Twenty-three years nine months and twenty- one days still fighting to reveal my innocence.

Antonio

* * *

My name is Piante and I would love to share my testimony of my journey and growth since I've been incarcerated and joined the Family Is First Project. I would like to share where I'm from and how I got here to begin with.

I'm from Cinti, oh born and raised by a strong black mother of 8 and I'm the 2nd oldest of three brothers and sisters and was blessed to grow up with them all under one roof. We lived in the low-income housing unit, and my mom worked every day. Even though we didn't get everything we wanted, we had everything we needed. My Grandma was a big blessing and was with us every day of my whole life. My mom and grandma didn't smoke, drink, or do drugs so we were blessed for that, but I had friends that had to go through that.

My only male role models were my uncles. One played sports and danced, the life of the party type person, and the other was into the streets and women, another life of the party. If you know me, then you know where I get my personality from. I'm calm, cool and aggressive. I love to joke and laugh as much as I can every day to this day. I believe I had a rough but fair upbringing. I always had a choice to do the right or wrong things in life. Did I do wrong? More than you can imagine, but I tried to live righteous every day.

A part of my wrongdoing days, I would hang on corners, sell drugs, carry guns, smoke weed, all of the reckless things we do as young, misguided men trying to come up. I've lost so many people to gun violence and prison; I knew I was headed to one or the other, maybe both. Well one day my number was called. By that, I mean I got into a situation where it was my life or his. No disrespect to the deceased nor his family, but the tables could have easily been turned and he could be sharing his testimony and me deceased. Really.

I mean 0.08 of a second changed my life forever. Well, in return, I received an 18yrs to life sentence. I missed out on my last child being born and I'm a father of 8 also. Since I been incarcerated, I've lost a few good friends I called my brothers. My oldest passed away 10-10-21, and the mother of my children is fighting breast cancer alone, It's a lot. It's enough to drive you insane, but only if you let it. When I first got incarcerated, I almost let myself go and gave up on everything, myself, and my family as well. I looked around and asked myself, why do so many children grow up without a father or a male role model present? And why are prisons filling up so fast with Black men? Young Black men; not only that, but all men.

During my incarceration I received a flyer that read, The Family Is First Project, with a signup sheet attached. So, I decided to sign up not knowing what to expect. We were then sent passes once a week, looking back I know that this was the best thing I've done since I've been in prison. I remember the first couple of classes, I would sit in the back of the class mad at the world, thinking, what am I doing here and why did I come.

I didn't know that Apostle Stacie always made it her business to call on those who sit in the back of the class when she was teaching because she knew that people who sit in the back like to hide. So, of course, she picked on me. She knew I had purpose and greatness within me! That when I really got to meet a real Queen, a woman so focused, determined to wake up and pour into young men it was unbelievable!

She not only gave us game on life, but she also gave us game on self. She showed me that life was more than just me and my current situation. She showed me that men have feelings and emotions and how to control them. She explained how roles get reversed and how women are forced to become the men of the household when we are not around. I now understand the true meaning of family. Family isn't just the same bloodline. Sometimes they will be the one that hurt you the worst. Family builds you and helps mold you, family teaches you to invest in genuine love, unconditionally. Family doesn't have ulterior motives for being in your corner. Family to me means those who really love and care about me unconditionally.

Apostle Stacie also showed me that I might not be sh** in the eyes of my haters, but I'm a Diamond to somebody out in the world. She helped me figure out if I'm a liability or an asset. Which one or you? The Family First Is Project is much more than a program; it's a way of life. Apostle Stacie is a Queen to me because everything she poured into me I can in return pour into someone else. Now I know what emotional intelligence is. I now know that everything I do has collateral damage. Once I graduated her first class of beginners, I became part of the alumni and that is when she taught us about being a real leader, a kingdom man! I feel like she left me with an invincible chain that I collect jewels in every day.

Believe it or not it's a lesson in front of you every day and it's up to you to understand and receive the blessing. It's so much that Apostle Stacie has opened my eyes to I have no choice but to see the truth and the light even with my eye lids shut. I promise if you give The Family Is First Project one shot, just one chance and apply the knowledge Apostle Stacie gives you, a lot of stress and strongholds will be lifted and loosened up off you. Your vision will become clearer, and you will begin to operate as a better person.

Even today, as of 12-25-21. Happy holidays to everyone. I can wholeheartedly say, I'm incarcerated, still facing 18yrs to life, or 10yrs to my parole date; but guess what? I'm still happy. I'm glad I found myself and my purpose in life. I now know the man, the father, the leader, and the teacher that lies within me. I am who I have to be for my youth and my Family.

Apostle Stacie Johnson, our Queen. The Family Is First Project/community means much more to me than you can imagine. It helped me with skills that were very much needed like communication, co-parenting from behind bars, self-control, solving money problems and setting and accomplishing my desired goals. I put a side criminal thinking, bad habits and putting myself in bad situations. Becoming a whole man is what Apostle Stacie helped me accomplish and for that I'm her diamond forever. I hope that reading this sparks a flame in you and you join our community of The Family Is First Project and you become one with your dear loved ones. Thank you always and forever

Thank you,

Piante

CHAPTER TEN

NCCI- THE VOICES

A WORD IN SEASON to you Apostle Stacie Johnson & your team... I first meet you at MTC. You and your team were doing a four-day conference... And before that I have heard so many good things about you through "The Long Term Offenders Program" from some of the guys I knew... So when " The Family Is First Project " started it was a must I be there... For one I could see the anointing on you and your team... I will never forget Evangelist Katina. She sang a song and it was like the Glory of Lord just filled the room instantly.

It was like she could see chains being broken, she started weeping & so did I ... In my journal that evening I wrote something down called The Vision Being Manifested...So now I want to share a word the Lord gave me through a vision... June 4, 2020. I saw these doors with locks on them. The Lord was speaking to me saying it takes faith to open them. But the Lord said Robert not any level of faith can open any door. According to Matthew16:18-19, I'm going to reference gates to DOORS. Jesus said the gates of hell shall not prevail against it. Then the Lord told Peter, I will give you the keys of the Kingdom of Heaven... When I read a vision that I had previously wrote down this year the Lord took me back to a vision I had previously wrote in May of 2015. Where I saw a keychain with a lot of skeleton keys on it... Later because I wanted to know what the Lord was saying, I asked the Lord and he said Robert, you can have a chain full of keys... But, just like now you can have the keys to walk out of this prison. But if you don't know which one opens what door, you still cannot get out of prison.

Then the Lord had me to look at the doors. Each of the door locks were color coded... And even though the guards work and have the keys. They are still of no use if they don't know what they have or don't understand their authority. Plus, the higher the authority you have the more access you have, just like the sergeants, captains and up to the Warden. So, the higher your authority is the more you can access. Amen, Apostle Stacie Johnson, the Lord says you have been given those Keys. With the Authority to set the captive free and build the Kingdom of Heaven. And from this point on let nothing I mean nothing stop you from doing what the Lord has called you to do...

Because nothing can stop you if He has spoken it...Amen and I know you hear the voice of the Lord because the first time you and your team came in July 28, 2017.... I listen to the word you were speaking to the men... When you were ministering and calling some to the fivefold ministry. And as I heard, I was in agreement with what the Lord was giving you... You and another member from your team called me the prophet... I was sure of who I was in the ministry... It was kind of funny Evangelist Loretta ask me one day after Family First, do I know who I am? I told her yes, she said are you sure? I said, I am sure. She said OK then prophet. Now I would just like you to know... Three out of the five you called to the Five-Fold Ministry are flowing in the ministry...So, please know that prison ministry is needed. Plus, you are called to this ministry. So again, The Family Is First Project was so many things to me, connecting us back to family and how to maintain a relationship with them.

So, this is what I also seen in the spirit. God used you to help the men understand who they are, and I thank for you not making it about just Christians, because the family is first project brought in men from other faiths and backgrounds that would have never come in if it was about only Christians. You made it about building leaders and lasting relationships with family and one another. We learned what it really meant to be my brother's keeper. Apostle Stacie, remember the Keys or should I say the Authority the Father has given you because you have a great ministry and the anointing on your life is powerful... You are a Kingdom builder Mighty Woman of a God...

Blessings,

Robert

* * *

I was born Walter. I didn't understand why at the age of four, my mother changed my name to Patrick. That was my first memory. My second memory was being molested by my older brother's friend. I was still only four, so the trauma of that act would cause me to forget it for many years. At the age of 10, I learned that I was adopted and so were all of my other siblings. Learning that news after I had established what I thought was a foundation of familial trust, devastated me. As a naive child, I felt that my parents, as loving as they were, were not my "real" parents, and my siblings were not my "real" siblings. I felt betrayed, isolated, in search of relationships that made me feel accepted. By the age of 15, I would find those relationships (or so I thought) in the form of sexual obligations to older men.

By the age of 18, I had graduated from high school and went away to college. Over the next few years, I had joined the Army, traveled the world, and accomplished great personal achievements. I had made my parents proud, became a role model for my younger siblings, and became an active and positive contributor in my community. I had it made, on the outside. On the inside, I was hollow. I had created an appearance of life that satisfied everyone around me, but my soul was lost. I didn't' understand my "self." I did not know why I struggled with so much inner turmoil; such a lack of self-worth; loneliness; and self-hatred, but I maintained the outer image because I never thought anyone would accept my inner truths.

Then, in 1993, my older sister was murdered by her estranged husband in a murder/ suicide, at my parent's home. My life was never the same after that. I felt the need to step up in life to help my elderly parents as they raised my sister's two daughters. I laugh today as I think about stepping up at that time, in somebody else's lives when I couldn't even step up in my own life, which gradually began to unravel. Drinking became my thing.

As I tried to be more responsible for my parents, I became less responsible for myself. I missed work and got fired. I missed classes, so was forced to set out a few quarters. I got evicted from my apartment and had to move in with a friend. To compensate for the loss of income, I got involved in the drug game and other criminal activities. Within a few years, my outer turmoil's which began to match my inner turmoil's had come to a head. I was convicted of multiple crimes and sentenced to life in prison.

At that time, I believed my life was over. No one in my family had ever been incarcerated. I had let everyone down. I felt tremendous guilt and shame. I pulled completely away from my family to live or die alone. Thoughts of suicide were a constant. An "I don't give a care" attitude was my mantra for life. This is how I lived for the first five years of my incarceration, until my pain became so deep that I was convinced I would kill myself. The thing is, no matter how destroyed I felt, I did not want to die. For the first time, I chose to share some of my pain with a friend. He suggested I get involved with a 1-year residential treatment program offered at the prison I was at. I signed up and was moved to the program. That decision established an entirely new perception of life for me, a life of self-awareness and self-healing.

In the program, I learned about stress management and anger management; about being aware of what is going on with "self" and learning tools to begin the long journey toward healing "self." I remembered being molested as a child and began to uncover the tremendous trauma that experience created in my mind. I learned about the abandonment issues that adoption creates for even a child adopted at six months of age. I learned that I am what I think I am, no matter what pretty picture I paint for the world. Therefore, it is important to think positive about myself and be the master of my thoughts. There is so much I learned through rehabilitative programming. After that year, I went from program participant to being a Program Aide, sharing my deepest and darkest secrets in service to others. This is how I met Pastor Stacie Johnson, thirteen years later. Eighteen years into my bid, I had become emersed in creating and facilitating multiple programs toward transforming lives in the prison community.

My life had never experienced so much joy than having this purpose and meaning of giving in an area in which I could relate with so much knowledge and passion. The only thing missing was, outside of prison, I had no one to share this joy with. I had become estranged from my family, partially by choice. My mother and father had both passed. Occasionally, I would talk to them and some of my siblings and nieces, over the phone, but I had not seen a single family member since my initial incarceration. My siblings and even my nieces had children that I had never met. As blessed as my life had become behind bars, I still had not dealt with my issues of guilt, shame and even abandonment when it came to my family.

In 2014, I signed up as a participant in The Family Is First Project being offered at the institution I was at. I understood that the premise of this project was to bridge the gap between incarcerated offenders and their families. I had gotten to a place in my development where I wanted to reconnect with my family, but I wasn't sure if I was ready for that. What was most scary is, I was not sure if my family was ready for that. When I first met Apostle Stacie Johnson, I felt insecure. She was an Apostle, and I was different. I had bad experiences with religious people because of my differences, so I anticipated that this project would not work for me. I was wrong. Apostle Stacie made me feel welcomed, even after I expressed to her how I was different.

Within the first couple of classes, I could see that she saw all of us as her brothers in Christ, which expanded my spiritual heart. When Apostle Stacie shared her personal journey of pain; love; loss and overcoming, it made me even more open to the possibilities this project would offer. We began with self-reflection and self-healing. Looking at who we were within our families before incarceration, who God created us to be as men within our families, and who we are today as incarcerated men in our families. That period of learning was very difficult because we were forced to uncover so many misconceptions of "being a man" that we had established. For many of us, we learned that we were still wounded little boys, portraying an unclear image of what it is to truly be fathers, husbands, boyfriends, sons, brothers, and uncles.

We learned about the many unhealthy ways we applied these portrayals of "men" into our families, poisoning the roots of our familial foundation; then Apostle Stacie took us on a path of healing ourselves and mending that family structure. The next phase of The Family Is First Project was Apostle Stacie and her team working with our families on the outside, via classes; phone conversations; and video conferences. The family work portion of this project helped our families to identify their proper roles in the family structure and established a foundation for families to learn to rebuild bonds despite incarceration.

The final stage of this project merged the offenders with their families through a series of classes. This stage was the most impactful for me. The first class of this stage took place in the institution's visiting room. There were about 30 inmate participants, and most of their families had already arrived. There was a happiness that I felt when I saw my fellow class members embracing their wives, girlfriends, children, mothers and even fathers. Some were even visited by siblings and grandparents. There was so much love in the room, it could be felt. While my sisters and nieces had been participating in the project with Apostle Stacie and her team by video conferences, I had little hope that they would travel four hours from our city to participate in this class. After all, I had not seen them in eighteen years. The class had begun. Families were sitting with one another, eating good food, participating in activities, and truly feeling Pastor Johnson's ministry of mending bonds between offenders and their families.

I was moved by her message but not moved enough for the message to change me the way I could see it was changing my fellow participants. My family had not come. I smiled and portrayed a very supportive image, but inside, I was hurt. I felt alone, abandoned, unworthy, unloved. I really wanted to cry, and I knew that I would do just that once I was able to get back to the privacy of my cell. I had achieved so much, in spite of being incarcerated, but I had no family to share that experience with. In that moment, I decided to take care of myself and not depend on anyone else for my happiness. As I began to let that proclamation settle into my heart, I looked up to notice our Staff Advisor staring in my direction, with a wide smile. I smiled back and waved at her uncomfortably, thinking that she must really be enjoying this class today. Then she pointed at me.

That's when I realized she was directing a group of people in my direction. Their body shapes had changed, and their ages had advanced, but their faces were still the same. My visitors were two of my younger sisters and my two nieces, the daughters of my sister who was killed years ago. Each of my nieces had brought their sons who I had never met. That day was the beginning of new and incredibly strong bonds between me and my family that have supported me through the past eight years of challenges in coping with long-term incarceration. This journey has not been easy for me as someone serving life in prison and I understand that it has not been easy for my family as they face the many challenges of life. However, I am grateful to Apostle Stacie and her Family Is First Project for making it possible and providing the tools for me and my family to face these challenges together.
Thank you for being God's Faithful Servant!
Patrick

***

My story on The Family Is First Project, I would like to start by how The Family Is First Project change my life. I was married before I came to prison, a family man with three lovely daughters but when the year of incarceration started to add I lost my wife and daughters and additional family, I felt lost and alone. Prison has a way of making you feel left for dead and isolated. believe me when I say I was lost without my family (daughters). So, years went passed in prison, while in prison I fasted and prayed to God asking him if he would restore my family back to me.

More years went by and one day they move me to a prison NCCI, while doing the same thing fasting and praying for my family, I heard about The Family Is First Project and at first I didn't believe the things they was saying about seeing your family and being able to connect with them while we are incarcerated, so I decided to join the program in spite of my inner thoughts of unbelief. Well surprisingly, Apostle Stacie and her group of women of God found my daughters and during our first family meeting I seen my daughter Gina Rose for the first time 15 years. as a father I didn't know what to say to her I didn't need to because she did all the talking, telling me how much she miss and loves me, and she told her sister where I was and later they came to see me their father and my family is growing spiritually.

We have bible study on the phone and we now fasting and praying over the phone as a family should. Because of The Family Is First Project my family is close to me and now I have some a new addition to my family three granddaughter's wow!!!!!! Thank you so much for everything and may God bless you.

your brother in the Lord Jesus Christ

Roy Gene jr.

***

Apostle, great grace and peace to my beloved sister in the Lord. I wanted to share a little bit on the experience I had partaking in your Family Is First Project. As a vessel, God used you to bring together a group of broken men and start the process of not only allowing the Holy Spirit to heal us but our families as well. When I first met you at the first revival here at NCCI. I was a Five Percenter who thought I was my own god. By the second revival, I was a born-again believer, and a big part of that was the Family Is First Project and seeing walking epistles living the gospel.

I am amazed that some of my closest friends and now brothers were men I met in that class. Every week I was excited to be able to dig into the Word of God and come together and discuss such relevant topics. The highlight was the family visit where for the first time in 20 years, I was able to visit with both of my sisters and my mom.

I have to say, till this day, Patrick, Dave, Jason, Roy, Josh, Rob, Ken, to name a few, are all my brothers. Most importantly, I met Rondall F. in that class and for the next year I studied under him. He is my spiritual father. Now, T.r.a.p.p. free bible study and the Love Walk are in every dorm on this compound, making weekly impact for the kingdom; thousands of men are giving their lives to Christ, and counting. I want to say thank you Apostle for your obedience to His Word to visit those in prison, and I want you to know that you as a vessel set in motion, with millions of families to be impacted by the Gospel. I will fill you in on more in due time.

Thanks for the revivals and all we were able to do for the kingdom. Thank you for prophesying over my life in the last kingdom event you held here. I am humbly growing into my purpose as a teacher, evangelist, and prophet. On behalf of all the men impacted for the better here at NCCI, I say thank you. The time is now to come back?? A lot has changed. Regardless, keep serving and loving and living for the King's return. We will continue to cover you in prayer. So, thank you and everyone you brought into minister to us. I pray our Father keeps blessing your ministry abundantly in Jesus name Amen. I'll be home this year and we have a lot more kingdom impact to do. I exit in great grace and peace from your beloved brother in Christ,

Antonio

***

When I first came to prison, I did not know what to expect or how my family would be affected by it. At the time, I did not realize the importance of family and how easily we can take them for granted. I also did not realize how much stress and pain my family would go through. Missing my family has been hard on me, especially with losing a loved one. But I met Apostle Stacie Johnson and The Family Is First Project. Not only was it a pleasure and an honor to help facilitate the program, I also learned a lot that helped me to appreciate my family more. It taught me how to cope with being in prison. It also helped me to appreciate my mother more.

I thank God for my mother. She has been my backbone and my supporter. Since The Family Is First Project, I lost my grandmother and her sister (my great aunt). The death of my grandmother devastated me. But, with the tools and skills The Family Is First Project taught me, I was able to reflect on those tools and apply them to what I was dealing with. It helped me get through those tough times. Thank you, Apostle Stacie Johnson, and The Family Is First Project.

Patrick

***

I've been in prison for 16 years. I was 18 when I got here. To describe this journey in one word. challenging. But life isn't about the challenge, it's the response that is most important. That's what separates the boys from the men and determines whether or not you overcome your circumstance, or your circumstance overcomes you. By the grace of God and with the help of Adonai Ministries/Mrs. Stacie I've been on the overcoming side of this challenge. A bunch of factors come into play when I think of how I'm making it. my family, friends, my brothers in the struggle with me and countless other factors. But the experiences I've had with my Adonai Family, it has shaped me more than I think they realize. I remember the first time I met Stacie and Frank. I was like 20 years old, still street minded and misled but determined to be better somehow some way. Lebanon Correctional opened the chapel to whoever wanted to come. I gave it a shot not knowing what to expect but hoping for a change and to my surprise that's exactly what I found.

I sat in a pew and listened to a man by the name of Frank Johnson share his story of how he overcame the penitentiary and the streets. I listened to him talk about doing time behind the same walls I was in and how he made his mind up to live different and answer the call on his life. It was mind blowing to see a man who walked in my shoes make the change he made. But what stood out the most was how his wife rode with him through his transition. It's the perfect story that inspired me to believe that God could do the same for me. Every brother in the joint is hoping for a lady like that to support him at his lowest. And to hear how they actually did it, was amazing. How they actually went through what we went/are going through.

They got married in prison, got out and continued to rock. They started their own ministry together, got blessed with a church and just continued to build and grow together. I ain't heard NOTHING like it NEVER! It was unbelievable, if it wasn't for me witnessing it myself, I probably wouldn't believe it either. Every time they hosted a service damn near the whole prison would show up. Bloods, crips, GDs, Muslims, Christians, and atheists. everybody came to see Stacie and Frank do they thang. You couldn't even find a seat. Up until then I never really felt God in a building.

That was an experience I was new to and to get it in the worst prison in Ohio amongst my savages was crazy! I ain't looked back since. Yeah I still have my struggles and I'm still here in prison waiting on my miracle. (that day when God says it's over son you can finally go home). but I damn sho ain't who I use to be, and I can thank Adonai Ministries for playing their role in that. I got my security level lowered in 2014 and left Lebanon and got transferred to Madison Correctional. Then I was transferred to North Central Correctional.

Thinking I would probably never see them again, guess who I ran into? Apostle Stacie Johnson. It was like a faith charge to see the woman who played such a major role in my growth. I instantly pledged myself to whatever vision she had. If I could be a part of it then that's exactly what I was going to do. I don't consider myself to be a religious person because I don't like religious people that just go through the motions and routines of "spirituality".

I like real people who do real things, especially when it's associated with my Creator and Apostle Stacie and her crew are just that and I'm with them all the way. Just like they came through Lebanon and rocked it, they did the same here at North Central. They restored families, I got brothers who hadn't talked to their kids and the mothers of their kids in years, then all of a sudden Apostle Stacie made it happen. Those people really care. They don't just TALK about it, they ARE about it. They exemplify what it means to be like Jesus. They actually showed up and showed out EVERYTIME they came through. And what's so powerful about what they do is they do it while going through major issues in their personal lives. They don't let setbacks and mishaps get in the way of the goal. They are determined to change lives no matter what! My life is a life amongst many that can prove that what they do is real. I love em I and I'm devoted to em for as long as I live.

Keep prospering.

Jamin

SPOKEN WORD

Title: I'm Free

I've been taken away, now I'm making a way.
It's a war going on, I can't just sit and play,
Its power in your tongue, watch what you say
Your future can be pleasantly, off of what you say today
I'm free, It won't cost you nothing
I'm free, without charge, I'm free indeed
I'm on to something....
I'm not about to speak myself in some more bondage
Money is nothing to me, give me some more knowledge
The voice of the truth is upon you
It's not about what they call you
It's about what you respond to
They attacked me with separation from my family
And a lack of communication
and then hit me with that modern segregation
I can't vote, I work for less, I'm considered less
And I supposed to accept all of this and sit and be depressed
Nah scratch that, I'm a father figure
I'm a king, I'm the President
I turned my cell into the oval office
I'm grabbing my max well early, its drinking coffee
This confidence is like common sense
I'm well qualified, but I use to be incompetent
I'm not what they say I am
I am what I say I am
Until I meet the great I am

I'm going H.A.M. (Hard As A Man)
Growth is the evidence of life
That's Why I'm steady growing
When I'm on the phone, My family says " I sound Free"
My response is " You better know it"
I been down bad in them trenches
I got scars to show it,
But: I'm alive and I'm well, I thank God for it
I'm thinking inside this box
I use to sit at the table with animals like Goldilocks
A few snakes, just to say the least
I will cut my neck off before I be on a leash
I'm out of bounds, so you can't confine me now
I'm the person, place, and thing, the whole noun
These affirmations gives me leverage, I'm levitating
Walking it out, step by step, I'm not into racing
Why? I been taking away, now I'm making a way
It's a war going on, I can't just sit and play
Its power in your tongue, watch what you say
Your future can be pleasantly
Off of what you say today

By Charles - CW

Love is the dove of peace, the spirit of brotherhood.

CHAPTER ELEVEN

LOCI – THE VOICES

S PIRITUALLY MY NAME IS YEEZ-RAL, meaning offspring of the Most High God, the Hebrew spelling of Jezreel, a son of his thundering. I was born May 7, 1968, after the will of the flesh to my mother and father son of an unknown man, in sin did my mother conceived me, fleshly living defines what led me inside the belly of incarceration. A place of violence and oppression where in this concrete box surrounded by double razor wire fences the voice of my heavenly father spoke through the darkness so powerfully, gently transforming who I am. I was lost growing up as a child, consciously of only loveless relationships and deceit.

151

I was raised to know that there was a God and that his son Jesus died for the sins of the world. Resurrected with all power in his hands, but circumstances surrounding my existence blocked opportunities earlier in my childhood that have a personal relationship with him. As a man child a legal adult I was a taker, if I saw it I wanted it somehow I got it. I could be charming, and I could be very aggressive. My appetite for alcohol, drugs, and sex was demanding, motivating my actions, feeding the darkness, the sin nature within me. I wanted to die when I realized I caused the death of another human being and was about to be arrested; though I had family, emotionally there were no emotional ties as I sat caged and afraid acknowledging the shame that I brought up on my family name looking out the window as it rained, I heard Abba's voice for the first time.

That was November 19, 1988. His voice spoke to me telling me to speak to my mother of all people telling her, it's going to be all right. Immediately I called my mother telling her those exact words not knowing as Abba spoke to me, he placed inside of me a seed of faith, though the germination process had not began, destiny was spoken concerning his plan for my life. Being caged, I consciously had to observe my past actions, which led me here, choices that entrap me, and the authority now that held back my destructive ways of living. The cataclysmic events that caused my arrest, being bounded, and chained, locked away from mainstream living was necessary.

The removal of the toxic circumstances flowing through my blood and mind had to run their course, the devouring process that dominated who God knew I would one day be had to be stopped. Judgment was declared. I was sentenced to serve 50 years to life in prison for causing the death of another human being. Unable to see a life after the age of 70, I angrily set out to survive. Yes, my family started this journey with me, but most of them have written me off for dead by their actions; they have gone on with their lives. I couldn't depend on no one. I was alone. It was Jan 23, 1994, that I realized that I wouldn't be able to survive if I continue living the way I was living inside of prison. I was gambling, drinking alcohol, smoking weed, and fighting both with the men that I was caged with and my overseer's authority. Tired and weary of this life sentence, at around 2:30 am I spoke to God, asking him to come into my life, to take control; and at that point I surrendered to His will concerning my life. In that moment, not knowing what it meant, I was translated from the power of darkness into the Kingdom of His light; a citizen of God's Kingdom.

Under the tutelage of His Holy Spirit, though it has taken many years, he has taught me to speak, to roar; thundering now, I represent Him here on earth, and as ambassador of Hs Kingdom, and for His Glory, I'll now testify of what he has done in my life up to this point. As I grew spiritually in wisdom, knowledge and understanding under the teaching of the Holy Spirit, I had to learn the importance of authority and how to operate in godly character which pleases God, and man. My entire belief system went through a reconstructive makeover.

The word of God challenged my every thought, and I was determined to line up to the constitution of His kingdom, which is love. My eyes opened for the first time to how my words and actions affect people, I became very quiet and still; but watchful, alert to the voice of God enlightening me and how to move in love amongst the people. Prison is a concentrated spot of people from all walks of life, addressing fears on a daily basis while passing through an atmosphere of condensed hatred, violence and mind-altering realities, which at any moment of weakness emotionally, any peace found could be interrupted by someone that, as myself, has been shipped to this place with life-rage, and my ways of operating doesn't sit well with their plans of survival.

I was forced to stand face to face with my pride, and the pride of others to realize that if I did not humble myself, I'd be stripped of all ability to fight to survive. My overseer's authority trumped my independent strength; physically, I had to take a backseat as I was taught how to operate in agape love effectively. Realizing that all authority has a higher authority to answer to. And Abba father authority was and is above all, and also, a desire to read the holy scriptures and sing songs of praise to Abba father came alive within me. I joined the congregation of God's people at a local institution at that time of incarceration. My job assignment was cleaning ovens in the kitchen every other evening after chow was served. As I carried out my duties, I sang, and as I sang, other men sang along with me, but there were those who complained; but God gave me favor with my overseers.

I was promoted to work as a porter in the institution, operating in buildings which house the offices of the high authority. As the process of my growth continued, I was now working for the warden, Maj., Capt., Lieut., and their secretaries. God's favor was impressed beautifully towards me as I walked in the understanding of the teaching of his spirit having learned so much yet feeling so out of place; reasoning with myself this can't be my purpose? Feeling myself being drawn away, I took a position that I had inquired in as a porter in a resident treatment unit were men dealing with mental health issues whereas not knowing for the next 21 years the glory of Abba father would receive as he used me, his son, in a mighty way.

When I started my new position as a porter, my responsibilities were to clean the hallways, bathrooms, and offices of all doctors, nurses and activity therapist, and their secretaries. It didn't take long to gain their respect, and as much trust that I had expected as an incarcerated man working so close to women on a daily basis before small acts of kindness that can only be described as God's favor, would appear. On days when I would finish my chores early, I started volunteering my time to assist with the program aid for the activity therapist during recreation periods for the men housed in the unit. And on days the program aid had visits and was scheduled to assist, the therapist would ask for my help. It was then that I realized this job assignment is where my life would have purpose. The men housed in that unit were special and everyone in the building made me feel welcome as I did my chores and help facilitate groups such as arts and crafts, socialization, bingo, letter writing, movie time, and music appreciation.

After a month or so of volunteering my time in the unit, I was approached one day by the administrative activity therapist who shared with me the reports of my volunteer time that the other therapist spoke highly of my interaction with the men and how the men responded, and how they would like to promote me as a recreational aid to assist the therapist and facilitate groups.

Gratefully, I accepted the job offer. As I continued singing Abba's praise, the light of his countenance shine through me as I walked in agape love sharing the joy, he gave me with everyone in the building. Why facilitating music appreciation, I developed the skill to play the piano. The men and I, with the permission of my supervisors, formed the choir, singing songs of inspiration and praise. I wrote songs, played; we performed musicals for the staff in the prison population. Also, I sang in the men's chorus that sang in the World Choir Games that came to Cincinnati, winning gold certificates in the categories of Spirituals and Gospel Music.

I was trained to be a minister to offer spiritual and emotional support to incarcerated men as myself. I was sent to an institution to attend a ten-day seminar to be certified to facilitate mental technology, teaching a class on habits, attitudes, beliefs and expectations are formed in the mind. To this day, having departed from that prison on July 15, 2017, I was promoted to program aid at another institution. I now facilitate two classes of mental technology on the transition treatment unit and others in the college hall. I also work in the chapel. I have co-directed the family choir, teaching songs of worship and praise graciously thundering glory as I am taught by my heavenly father.

I want to thank Apostle Stacie Johnson for the opportunity to participate in the Family is First Project and to share my story that there is still hope while incarcerated. I want to thank the Family Is First Project for their dedication, the love, the commitment and speaking truth. To all the men and women that are reading this book, there is still light at the end of the tunnel.

Forever grateful,
Mark

Job 37:5 *God thundering marvelously with this voice, great things do with he, do with he which we cannot comprehend*
Hosea 1:4 *And the Lord said unto him call his name Jezreel*

* * *

December 11, 1995, I'm in the back of a police car handcuffed and shivering from the intense cold fear of a possible life sentence for robbery and murder I just committed the day before. I had never thought about the consequences of my actions up until this point; I had never thought about the effect my actions have on my loved ones up until this point. So, it was of no surprise when my selfish and self-centered ways took over and I went right back to placing the blame elsewhere instead of accepting responsibility. If only my conditions at home as a child were different, I would not behave the way I do. If my mother wouldn't have put me out of her house, I would not have been in the streets in the first place.

All he had to do was give me what I came for and I would not have had to shoot him. Despite my efforts to justify the destruction I've caused, I was guilty of this senseless crime, and 23 years of my life was my punishment. I was 18 years old, spiritually bankrupt, and totally oblivious to what had now become my reality. I was mad at the world and felt as if I was the only one who had been victimized. I was hurting inside and wanted to inflict the same hurt and pain on others, and for the next 17 years of my incarceration, I did just that. I was extremely manipulative. I lied; I cheated, stole and I used drugs and alcohol as a means to numb me, so I didn't have to deal with my feelings. I continued to blame my outlandish behavior on my childhood and upbringing, and I couldn't be convinced otherwise.

I was raised in the spiritual household, but I didn't understand faith. I never attempted to seek any understanding and when things didn't go according to my plans, I cursed God. I was too blinded, ignorant to see at that time, was that God had been sparing my life since the day I decided to jump off the porch and go out on my own. He placed me in here to sit me down because the life I was so anxious to live wasn't what he had planned for me, and no matter how hard I fought to operate in darkness, God's light was always present. I definitely didn't deserve the blessings that God began to bestow upon me, but they became abundant! He began to change the course of my life by allowing me to make the decision to start participating in my life in positive and productive ways. My eyes were opening a little and I was starting to see that I wanted more for myself than to just sit here in prison and wither away.

I decided to get back in school and obtain my GED and I even took some college classes for several semesters intending on obtaining an associate degree in Business Administration. I studied relentlessly and learned so much, but there still seemed to be this void in my life that needed to be filled, so I started to drink alcohol and smoke marijuana in access to fill the empty space in my heart and mind, hoping it brought about a sense of peace in the chaos that had become my life. I was reading any and everything I got my hands on, and I became particularly interested in books about my heritage: the African culture and the Rastafarian, and teachings and way of life.

I gravitated towards guys who are interested in these things as well and we spent the majority of our time together. I studied Psalms and other books in the Bible, and I'd listen to Bob Marley, Peter Tosh and other reggae artists. I had already stopped combing or cutting my hair so by now I had long flowing dreadlocks which allowed me to not only talk the talk but look the part as well. This newfound way of life had begun to create an identity in the fact that my marijuana use was now less frowned upon than it was to be expected, made me accept it even more. My level of maturity began to increase, and I was finally gaining confidence in myself. I no longer saw myself as a failure; I was somebody! I knew it would take a lot more words for me to figure out just who that somebody was, and I also knew I was done trying to be this person I thought I had to be to fit in or be accepted by people who really didn't even matter to me.

A family friend who I had written back and forth with for several years came to visit me and although we hadn't seen each other in over 16 years we hit it off instantly. Having gone without any female interaction physically, mentally, or emotionally for years, I was beyond anxious and extremely vulnerable. I yearn to feel loved and needed by someone. We had a real connection in our feelings for one another, and these feelings grew immediately. I finally had my Queen, and I wasn't letting her go. Not once did I take into consideration the fact that I had to go in front of the parole board and if given more time, I couldn't be there for her the way she needed me to be. Not once did I take into consideration her feelings, when I'm not there to protect her and provide for her the way I'm supposed to.

I was falling in love with her and nothing else in the world matter to me, I thought she just might be the one thing that could finally fill this void and I wasn't going to let this opportunity slip through my hands, so I poured it on thick and swept her completely off her feet. My manipulative, selfish, and self-centered ways was a repellent to any empathy/care or concern, and after a year of lusting over each other, whispering sweet nothings, and promising her the world, we got married. On the other side, it appeared that I had it all together. I had my head held high; walk upright, my shoulders back, chest out. I demanded everyone's attention when I entered the room, and even I was beginning to believe this is fictitious and frivolous mambo jumbo I masqueraded as intelligence. I talked about taking care of her and to prove to her I was willing and able to send money home from a few illegal transactions that I have promised her at the start of our relationship that I stopped doing only in my head.

This made it okay to accept her money and do with it whatever I wanted; she also sent clothes and food boxes regularly; put money on the phone and would travel up and down the highway to see me at least twice a month. I would always tell her how much I appreciated her but there wasn't much evidence to support what I was saying. I told her I was all about her, and I honestly believed I was but in reality, I was all about me and me only!

I wasn't making my deposits into our marriage; I only made withdrawals. She would let me know in subtle ways. but I couldn't see. I was focused on what I wanted. After all these years. I hadn't grown up. I was still the same 18-year-old kid that entered the prison system. The only difference was I now had a ton of information and certificates and I wasn't prepared to do anything with. Nobody could tell me anything and I had become so good at playing this role I was starting to believe the lie myself. I talked to my peers about what God was doing in my life, but in all actuality, I didn't have any type of relationship with God. I took the credit for the direction my life was now headed. I only called on God when I was in a situation that I needed him to get me out of, or when I wanted certain things to go my way; but as soon as I got what I wanted or not, I forgot all about him.

I didn't thank God for waking me up this morning and getting me through my day. I didn't ask God to bless those who I claim to love. And I definitely didn't ask God to bless those who I was in conflict with, and who I felt had done me wrong. I was gorging my carnal man and totally neglecting my spirit man, and I was comfortable with the façade. I thought I was preparing myself to go and live life as a cheater, con man, and criminal!

The time had finally arrived, and I was going in front of the parole board. I had to be sure I was ready, so I ironed my clothes, cut my hair, and showered; gathered up my certificates and had a dress rehearsal in front of the mirror. I waited with several other inmates, and when it was my turn, I went in and sat in front of the huge screen. Several board members were on the screen surrounding the table and as soon as the person conducting my hearing began to speak, I sank into my chair and became that lost, broken, abandoned, and neglected little boy all over again. I was put to the test, literally! They wanted to know my plans and how society would benefit from my release. They wanted to know where I would work and what I would do if I could find a job. I tried to answer their questions to the best of my ability, but my answers lacked sincerity and substance, and it was quite obvious I was ill prepared.

I could no longer use my creased clean cut outer appearance, slick pretentious mouthpiece, or the array of colorful certificates I collected as a smokescreen to hide the guilty and grimy interior. I had been exposed, and the end result was a five-year continuance. I was crushed! I curse God and begin to question him. How could you let this happen to me? I called on you in my time of need and you didn't answer; did you not hear me? Are you not who you say you are? Unbeknownst to me, God loves me and cares for me more than I love and cared for myself, and he never stopped working in my life. He is most definitely who he says he is, and it was a fact he will allow this to happen to me. God had a plan for me, and he wasn't going to allow me to walk out of this place anything less than the man he created me to be. Of course, I hadn't realized this just yet.

I was still playing the victim and I was just getting started on my pity party. I smoked marijuana the entire time while waiting for my parole board date and now that I have more time to do, I was definitely going to smoke every chance I got. I was attempting to make myself feel better, and to justify my drug use, I told myself and those who made an attempt at confronting my behavior that I needed to get high to escape the harsh reality of this mental and physical bondage I was a victim of. It never occurred to me that I was only adding to the stress, frustration and uncomfortableness associated with the situation I was currently in. I was given a urine test a few days after my parole board hearing and the reality I was so desperate to escape was once again smacking me in the face.

I was somehow able to avoid a dirty urine, and instead of me recognizing this obvious power greater than myself working to halt the self-sabotage that served to have become my norm, as usual, I believed it was something I did that allowed me to make it through this urinalysis unscathed. I decided to try something different, so I got involved with a recovery-based program that could keep me busy and possibly add to my list of accomplishments to impress the parole board next time. I didn't think I had a drug problem, and I had no intentions on stopping. I just want to slow down a little, and I figured this program could help me. My wife continued to love me, support me, and stay by my side in spite of me, and she encouraged me to use this time to work on myself.

I was willing to give it a try, and because the woman I loved and planned on spending my life with suggested, I was more inclined to sign up. I was moved to the recovery dorm three days before my 36th birthday and I wasn't necessarily ready to move at that time. I had saved a couple of joints and I plan on celebrating my birthday the way I always have since I was 15 years old, and that's exactly what I did! With little care or concern for the days in the dorm trying to recover from addiction, I partied right in the dorm. I couldn't understand why they were looking at me as if I had just committed the ultimate CM, and I didn't like it one bit. I actually felt foolish sitting in the recovery base housing unit high as a kite. The next morning, while brushing my teeth, I looked in the mirror, and at that moment, I realized I didn't like the person that was staring back at me. Here I was sitting in prison where I had spent half of my life.

I loathe this place and was absolutely sick of being here. I was doing my time as if I was the brick and mortar that the prison placed together. The decisions I made and the things I involved myself with here for the sole purpose of instant gratification. I wasn't thinking about my future, and I was totally unprepared for life after incarceration. My only concern was right now. Whatever made me feel good at that particular time is what I did. I had a wife who had put her life on hold and was counting on me to come home and be the man I promised her I'd be, but I didn't know the first thing about being a man.

My parents were growing older and older right before my eyes and are both dealing with health issues, and I'm in here squandering the chance to finally do something with my life that would make them proud. I barely knew my brothers and I felt like they had written me off, so I harbored resentment and hatred towards them. I wanted to be free more than anything in the world; however, getting high took precedence over everything in my life. I wanted to stop, if for no other reason, than to rid myself of the shame and guilt I felt every time I lied to my wife and mother about the things I was in here doing. It was clear that I had a problem, and I knew I wasn't going to be able to fix this problem on my own. I needed to get out of my comfort zone and become willing to allow someone to help me.

It was time for me to stop taking life for granted, put away those childish things, and become the man my wife and family needed me to be. As soon as the opportunity presented itself, I stood up in front of the entire community and held myself accountable. I told them that I had lied during my interview and screening and that I was still getting high. I asked them for their help and said I was willing to do whatever the program asked of me. To my surprise the counselors didn't scold me. Instead, they said that they respected me for it and it's a huge step towards making some changes in my life.

The whole "prison cold thing" was still ingrained in me so of course I felt weird standing in front of complete strangers telling on myself, but it felt like a huge weight was lifted off my shoulders and it seemed like I had done the right thing. I started treatment shortly after and was a little reluctant because I had no clue what I was getting myself into. My counselor and crew members help me identify and address some core issues. Abandonment, acceptance, and neglect had followed me from childhood into adulthood and instead of running from these issues it was time to face them. I had some deep wounds that have never been treated and infection had set in, so they peeled off the Band-Aid I had covered these wounds with and them scraping out the infection to irritate and clean the wounds so I would heal properly.

I was often unreceptive and couldn't stand the fact that these people who barely knew me were trying to tell me about myself. Although I sat in the same room as these men, wore the same blue prison attire, and our stories were parallel in so many ways, I felt I didn't belong here. I was nothing like these people! A few friends of mine that were already graduates of the program talk to me and help me see that we have more similarities than differences, and I was in fact a lot more like these men than I wanted to believe. The program talked about spirituality as opposed to religion and almost everything I heard or read pertained to God or a higher power. I needed all the help I could get, so I figured I'd stop fighting with God and start fighting for God.

I didn't know how to pray or meditate so I asked a lot of questions. I begin taking suggestions which help me become more open-minded to the process and it was evident that I had made the right decision. I finally had some structure in my life, and I was learning how to be responsible, honest, and sociable as well. My thinking was challenged daily, and my distorted belief system began to change. I was done blaming everyone else, and I had come to the realization that I play a big part in everything that happens to me. My part is the only thing I have the ability to control, and change is me, and I was learning to be okay with the things I couldn't control or change.

Each time I opened up and expose things about myself I was like an onion peeling away layer upon layer. I was also slowly removing the different mask I wore for so long that had helped my pseudo-self-maneuver through life undetected. I worked on my resentments and fears and made some mends to people I've harmed. I participated in the 12-step program and The Family Is First Project with my wife and parents and we went through group therapy with several other families.

This was one of the hardest things I've ever had to do in my life was to sit and listen to my wife and mother tell me about all the stuff I done to them that I thought they were too naïve to see, and how it made them feel. We laughed together and definitely cried together doing this process, but it was one of the greatest experiences I've had in my life. I was able to remove the last mask and finally reveal my true self and the people who matter most to me.

We became one big family, and I made some friends during this process who I will remember forever! Thank you, Apostle Stacie. I finally graduated from the 12-step program and was so appreciative of the program for helping me change my life and for restoring some of the relationships I had put so much effort into trying to destroy. I decided to stay in the dorm and be a program aid. I felt it was my duty and the least I could do to give back what was so freely given to me, and I had become accustomed to the structure that the program brought to my life. I had no desire to be around guys who were living how I was living and doing the things I was doing.

My relationship with God grew tremendously and I made it a priority to show him some gratitude through prayer, meditation and by nurturing the relationships he helps me to restore, as well as new relationships I had acquired along my journey. I felt so much better about myself. People began to see me as a leader, and I got so excited every time I got the opportunity to mentor a young man who was going through the same struggle I had gone through, and I watched him graduate and ultimately turn his life completely around. It blew my mind when guys began asking me to sponsor them and help guide them through the 12 steps of N.A. I've harmed so many people throughout my life, and people are actually looking to me for advice and trusting me with their deepest darkest secrets. It was an absolute privilege to help these young men, and the experience quite humbling.

People began to believe in me and want to help me because they can see that I believed in myself and was serious about my life. I got into Barber College, and by the grace of God and hard work and determination, I obtained my barber's license. My parole board date was approaching, and I was determined to be prepared for it this time. My family was anxious and certain this was my time. I was excited as well because I knew how much work I had put in. I had a strong support system inside and outside of prison; I have letters from several barbershops that were willing to hire me; I had support letters from family, friends, prison staff, recovery programs, halfway houses, and community leaders.

I had a five-year plan starting with my first day home, and I had a financial plan as well. I prayed to God and asked that his will be done and not my own. I asked him to remove all fears and allow me to walk into this hearing with confidence knowing that I'm not the same person they saw five years ago. I was totally honest with them about the crime I have committed, and I accepted full responsibility for taking this man's life. I express my regret and remorse and how the feelings of shame and guilt are no longer barriers in my growth because I had forgiven myself. The hearing went extremely well, and they were impressed with how prepared I was in my level of honesty. I was told they would have a full board hearing on my behalf and send my decision in the mail. My wife and family were ecstatic and had faith that this was finally it.

I was going to be free! I tried not to get my hopes up too high, but it seemed as if everyone was excited for me, and I felt it in my heart that I was going to be released. Nearly 2 months after my parole hearing the decision came and I was given another five-year continuance. I was completely heartbroken! My wife didn't show much emotion. I guess to show me that she's being strong but deep down I knew she was crushed and hurting. My mother tried to be strong as well, but the fact that I didn't hear from her for about a week let me know that she wasn't taking the news too well.

I felt as if I had put them through enough heart ache and pain to last a lifetime, and they didn't deserve to continue to go through this. I was overcome with depression, and I began isolating myself from everyone. My counselors pulled me in and gave me some words of encouragement, but I was dazed and confused and couldn't hear any of it. When I was by myself and nobody was around, my emotions took over and I cried uncontrollably. I wasn't getting much sleep because I was completely consumed by thoughts of spending my life in prison, never getting the opportunity to have and raise children of my own, not being able to experience life with my wife, and not getting a chance to let my mother see me be successful and live a good life before she passes away. While up at night, I had extensive conversations with God, and I had lots of questions. What is it that I'm not doing? What is my purpose for being here? Will I ever be free?

After several weeks of prayer and meditation and talking to friends and family about my thoughts and feelings the depression began to subside. I stayed connected with the program and was still of service to others through mentorship, sponsorship, the big brother/little brother process, and being a positive leader in the dorm. Old acquaintances would stop me on the yard and tell me I should leave this dorm and program because it didn't help me at the parole board.

I always smile and continue on my path with certainty that this program is what help me get out of spiritual bankruptcy and into a life filled with meaning and purpose. At times I wasn't sure if I could continue on this path, but God always found a way to remind me of the person I was, and what it took for me to be free of that person and that destructive lifestyle. My family continued to support me and encouraged me to keep walking this righteous path and insured me my time will come.

The affect that this time was having on my wife and marriage as a whole began to show outwardly and I wasn't so sure we could sustain the pressure associated with being in an abnormal marriage. I continue working on myself and I was determined to be the best version of me possible. I held strong on my faith in God and knew if he intended on the two of us being together nothing could come between us. I began to understand and realize that it is on His own time. It's not about how ready I think I am; I know God knows what's best for me.

And ever since I've allowed him to run my life and fully surrendered to his will and his way, great things have been happening. A year has passed since my last hearing, things not going the way I would have liked them, but I'm at peace today. I have since been chosen to be the institutions staff barber at a different prison. I have an opportunity to perfect my craft and make some decent money in the process. I'm also able to practice the things I learned along my journey and remain active in my king man role.

I'm now able to invoke change and utilize these spiritual principles I've gained to overcome the uncomfortableness that will come. By using the gift God gave me I'm able to boost others confidence and self-esteem, hone my skills, work on being sociable, and possibly make some connections that would be beneficial to my release. I'm not where I like to be in my life physically, but I'm mentally, spiritually, and emotionally happy. Today, I know that God is leading me in the direction that I should go; but ultimately, I control my own life. I am who I am because of the path I've chosen. I am not happy because I am well, I am well because I am happy. I have faith because my life is good, my life is good because I have faith.

Thank you so much Apostle Stacie,
Kevin D

CHAPTER TWELVE

BEHIND ENEMY LINES

Romans 8:28 And we know that in all things God works for the good of those who love him, who have been called according to his purpose (NIV.)

THINGS WERE FLOWING and it was full speed ahead. I was in three prisons teaching and facilitating with the Family is First Project. All together I had over 150 families connected to the program. When people looked at me, they would tell me that I was living my dream, and they were correct; I was! I was right in the flow and planning to take the vision higher. I had done an interview with our local news station Channel 5 here in Cincinnati, Ohio. I had written my first book, *While You Wait*, and in the interview, I talked about The Family is First Project and being a wife of an inmate, and the impact that The Family is First Project had on the families.

I had also completed my proposal to get the program into other prisons and had set me eyes on going into the Federal Prisons. I was ready and willing to launch out. I say this with all humility that God allowed me to create an army of strong men and women believers across the prison system and the Holy Spirit was moving. This was His army of faith-filled power believers who wanted to see their lives changed.

During my travels in the prisons, I have met some wonderful people: guards, chaplains and other staff that supported and believed in what I was doing. But there were also people who did not like the fact of a black woman coming into the prisons and making an impact. You know, when you are doing a work for the Lord there will always be opposition, jealously and hatred. It was in the spring of 2019 when my whole world started to crash around me. I remember like it was yesterday.

I was working full time and doing full time ministry, and for the record, let me just say that my day job was funding the ministry which allowed me and the team to travel, stay in hotels and provide the extras. Suddenly, there was a major layoff and now I was unemployed. The blessed thing about it was the employer gave the company workers a nice severance package which provided for a while. This allowed me to look for employment and still do prison ministry. I was not worried about getting another job because I knew that God was going to provide, and I also knew that it was in his timing. By this time, I had completed most of my college education and I was working on my Doctorate in Organizational Development and Leadership, so I was not worried about getting another job. I knew I had to wait until God placed me in the right one.

I was still in school pursuing my Doctorate degree. I had finally completed all the course work with A's and B's, and I was finally on the writing of my dissertation. I had been to Arizona and attended two residencies. I was meeting with my chair and things were still moving. I was at the point in my life where I was reflecting on how God directed me to go back to school after I had dropped out in the 10th grade so many years ago. I pondered on the blessings and grace he had given me to thrive so continuing my education was near and dear to my heart. One morning I received a call from my school advisor that I had ran out of finances and there was no more government money for me to continue. I tried loans. I tired borrowing the money.

I even tried talking with them to put me on a payment plan but to no avail. I only had six classes until completion, and now, no money. I was informed by my advisor that if I could not come up with the money, I had to self-pay, and until then they pretty much kicked me out of school and cut off my access to my chair and their website. It was a horrible moment for me because I had worked so hard. I felt like I hit a brick wall, and just when you think it could not get any worse, in that same week I received a call from one of the prisons volunteer coordinators who informed me that I was being investigated.

My thoughts at that moment were, *I'm good. I have nothing to hide. The Family Is First Project is squeaky clean.* In all my years of prison ministry I had never done anything inappropriate towards an inmate and I have never been disrespected by any inmate. This individual informed me that one of the sergeants, was out to get her because he did not like her; plus, she told me that they did not get along and he did not approve of all the positive things she was doing for the men in the prison. It's sad to say but you really have people who are like that, they don't want to see anything positive from behinds bars because that meant CHANGE!

You see, she was also a powerful woman making moves, building the men's self-esteem through the many programs she was hosting and bringing in. She was an open target, and the enemy did not like what was happening, and I just happen to be one of the programs under her. And not to mention, The Family is First Project was one of the biggest programs there. I had 40 men in the class and 12 facilitators. 40 men totaled 40 families that I was servicing.

So, when I got the call from her stating that the sergeant was investigating me, I was not worried. She went on to tell me that she overheard him talking to some other people and they were saying how they were going to try and shut my program down. When I got off the phone, I was a little disturbed, but I was not worried because I knew I had not done anything, plus I had built such a reputation with ODRC that it was untouchable, or so I thought.

Outside of running my program in three different prisons, I had conducted workshops, did presentations, and was a guest speaker for the penal system time and time again. The people in administration knew about me and what I was doing. Keep in mind, The Family is First Project had been running for 10 straight years, so I felt I had built a solid enough foundation. Not to mention, in my proposal I had testimonials from inmates and their families as evidence to show how the Family is First Project was impacting lives.

It wasn't until I received another call from someone else who told me that same thing; but this time, I was informed that this sergeant was calling around to all the prison asking questions about me and the program and that he was investigating me because I was Jpay-ing too many men. Jpay is inmate email, and I was always allowed to Jpay my alumni facilitators, before. This is how we communicated about the classes and program details when I could not be present. Being able to Jpay the inmates was also listed in the proposal and this particular prison had agreed to these terms when they accepted me to bring in The Family Is First Project.

So, I was a bit confused, but now concerned. I was informed that this male sergeant who never knew me and never attended any of the Family is First Project functions, would try and shut it down. I was told that he said I was in violation, because as a volunteer having contact with the inmates through Jpay was prohibited. I was told he said that I was doing too much, and he was going to stop me. He was also going to write a letter to upper management and request that my volunteer status be revoked indefinitely.

By this time, I was shocked that this was happening, I knew the rules but for the last 10 years this had always been allowed in the other prison, and at this particular prison I did ask permission. I had a hard time understanding why this person, whom I never knew, wanted to destroy me. I tried really hard not to take it personally, but this felt very personal. I knew I had made the devil angry with all that was happening in the prisons, I just did not know how angry he was. I know the enemy can use anybody, but I was caught way off guard with this one. So, I was informed that I should write a letter (email) to administration explaining my program and why I was Jpay-ing the inmates and I needed to do it quickly because this sergeant was about to send them an email requesting my removal. So, I typed the email and sent it quickly to administration.

I also made a phone call to administration and spoke to a woman who was the contact person at that time. She assured me that it was not going to be that bad, stating that it was just an email and she would read my letter, and if worse came to worse, I would only be suspended for a month until they resolved the matter. She promised that things would be fine.

I trusted what she told me because I had been faithful to my mission for 10 solid years, not missing any days. I labored to build a spotless reputation; especially being a woman going inside a male institution, I had to keep a clean record. Plus, this was my name and program on the line. This sergeant investigated me back the entire 10 years reading every single Jpay and he did not find a single inappropriate thing! But, in spite of my efforts to clear up this misunderstanding he sent an email requesting that I be suspended for one year.

When administration received his email, that same woman who told me everything would be ok, in turned sent a nationwide email to all the prisons stating that my volunteer status has been revoked and I was suspended for a year. I guess she had no choice, and she was just following procedure. When that email was sent out, my whole world changed. When the other prisons got that email, without question, they shut all my programs down. It did not matter if I was up and running; at that moment, I was not allowed to come in and preach or teach anymore!

The men and the families were left hanging and so was I. Major damage had been done and this was a blow I was not ready for. I could not believe that this man had this much power with one ink pen! A vision that took 20 years to build through labor, sweat, tears and much prayer was now gone. I called the prison to speak with this person, but of course, he would not return my calls. I called the deputy warden, who brushed me off. I called the warden who stated they would be investigating the incident and would get back with me.

This was not good at all. My world was crumbing right before my eyes, and they brushed me off as if I did something wrong. I called administration time and time again just to get voicemails and when I did reach someone, they were forever looking into it. Nevertheless, to say, nothing got done, and my name that had a spotless record was now stained with a falsified well-dressed lie!

I was blown away from the treatment I received from the people who I thought I was on the same team with for over a decade. No calls. No response. I was left in the dark while my program, my dream was dismantled. Brokenhearted and wounded, I tried time and time again to get answers, but the only thing that I was told when I called was, I was suspended for Jpay-ing inmates. This was shocking because they knew this, I had always asked permission and I would have never taken those liberties without approval! Nevertheless, here I was, in the deepest, darkest place that I have never been.

So, now I'm wounded and hurt, I'm thinking to myself, how can I be punished for something you knew about? For the first time in my life, I felt like some of the inmates I had been mentoring and teaching for so many years. I was treated as guilty before I could prove my innocence. You see, this sergeant and prison officials would not even sit down with me and discuss this like adults. I wanted a face-to-face meeting; bring my accusers before me and let them present their case because my defense was solid. I was innocent of all charges, and I was more than willing to stand before them and prove it. But to no avail, they would never meet with me or return my calls or emails, and when I spoke with administration it was more of them looking into the matter, I felt I got the ultimate brushing off.

By this time, the prisons had informed the inmates, I was hoping that they would at least explain in some detail what had happened. I did not want the inmates to feel as if I had just dropped them. But I thank God they know my character, I had built up such a rapport with the men and women they knew something was desperately wrong, that leaving suddenly was not of my doing. The men, and the families, were left hanging.

I tried to clean it up as much as possible, but I was hurting, wounded, and left with no answers as to why. People have always considered me to be a strong black woman and it takes a lot for me to cry; but this broke me! I cried for days and weeks seeking God and asking why? After all, this vision was my baby and I did not want to let it go.

I was so connected to the men and women and my prison ministry, I did not know how to let go, or why I had to let go. After all, I felt and know, I did not do anything wrong. It felt like I was in the darkest moments of my life. This was my baby, my vision, my purpose. I thought, *how do I move on from here?* I had just got three major blows in the same month that shook my whole world and I sat crying at times wondering how I would try to pick up the pieces. My husband Frank was my biggest encourager; he could see the hurt on my face and the wounds to my heart.

He supported me and stood by my side praying and encouraging me. My team was also crushed; they had been so blessed by the ministry they could not understand deceit on this level. You see, when the prison banned me, anyone associated with Adonai Ministries or the Family is First Project, was suspended. They were also investigated by this sergeant, and they were found guilty by association. It was ugly and cruel how things were done, and no matter how hard I tried, I could not stop it. This was one of those times I questioned God and asked why? I knew nothing happens unless God gives the approval, so why was the approval given on this one? Was I holding on too tight? What could I have done to be attacked so harshly that my entire ministry be dismantled? How could you let this happen God?

What about the men, the families? What about me? I'm being very transparent right now. I had to have a one-on-one talk with the Lord. I needed God, The Most High, The King of Kings, to help me understand and make it all better. I remember feeling empty as time passed on. One of the blessed things out of it was that WCI allowed me to finish my class and graduate the men out; they just did not leave them hanging like the other prisons did. But because of my suspension, after the graduation, I was not permitted to return.

I appreciate the grace I was given by WCI and the concern for the inmates and their families. I remember as I was seeking God, and doing a lot of reflecting, I received a call from one of the family members who wanted to purchase my newly written book, *While You Wait*. We met in the parking lot of a bank. When she spoke with me, she was so happy to be receiving my book, and before she pulled off, she told me to remember **Romans 8:28 that all things are working together for my good**. I smiled softly and told her thank you. While I was at home that same day, I was watching TV and this program came on that seemed interesting. It was called, *Manifest*. As I began to watch it, I kept seeing and hearing Romans 8:28. Huhhh??? Throughout the entire first show they were showing signs and talking about this scripture.

I knew this particular verse. My spirit began to jump, so, I had to go get my bible and open it up. I knew God was telling me something in the midst of my pain. So here is what the scripture says: **Romans 8:28, "And we know that in all things God works for the good of those who love him, who have been called according to his purpose" (NIV).** In the midst of my hurt and pain God said it was working for my good. I could not see how just yet, but I knew God was working something out in me. And when He said ALL THINGS, he meant ALL.

The good, the bad and the sure enough ugly. I knew then that God was going to get the glory no matter what! During the time of my seeking God and my growth and development. I heard through the grapevine that some of the men who I had been Jpaying, those who were in faith-based dorms where purposely placed back into population and I felt like just more darts were from the enemy being hurtled at us. This made me pray even harder. I felt I not only had to spiritually fight for me but also for them. This attack was heavy and deep, and it was set out to destroy. Oh, But God! God had a plan like no other. On top of all the betrayal and lies I had one more hurdle to jump. You see, my daughter, who had passed away years ago, I still had her stuff in storage and because I lost my job, I could not continue to pay the storage bill. I was holding on to her things for her daughters hoping they would want it, but so much time had passed most of the items were damaged and even ruined.

Frank was going to give me the money, but I decided to let it go. So, we planned to go clean out the storage and be done with it. I was in a better place with cleaning out her things and I remember when we were finished, I looked at the empty storage bin and I heard the Lord say, "Now your storage is truly empty." God had closed some major chapters in my life, and he told me that this was my year 10 of releasing things. According to the website, BibleStudy.org, the number 10 signifies: testimony, law, responsibility, and the completeness of order. So, I received what God was speaking in my spirit man that He was completing things in my life. What the enemy meant for evil God said He was going to turn it around for my good. Months had passed and I continued to reach out for answers and understanding. I tried to stay connected with the families, but it was very difficult with the prison piece dismantled. Plus, I was still hurting.

I remember I was once invited to be one of the guest speakers in a re-entry conference in Dayton, Ohio my one of my dearest friends Hope. I had an opportunity to share my story and tell about The Family Is First Project even though it was not up and running. Prior to this event, Hope introduced me to one of her friends who I had shared my story with. He was very interested in The Family Is First Project and wanted me to bring it into the jails in Dayton, Oh. I gave it some thought but I never made a decision, nor did I call him back. To be honest with you, I had so much going on and the thought of starting over, going back into the jails was not in the forefront of my mind. I looked at it as taking a step backwards. Plus, I felt the very wind had been knocked out of me.

I was not willing to start from scratch when I felt I had done no wrong. It just so happened that this same Chaplain was at the reentry conference. I found an opportunity to apologize to him and I told him I was still hurting from all the events that happened with The Family Is First Project. This man spoke some powerful words that I will never forget which helped open my eyes to inner healing. He told me that he honored my honesty, and He always tells leaders "It's hard to lead when you are bleeding." He knew from my story how deep my wounds went. Over the 25 years of prison ministry, I poured out my soul I gave my last and I loved unconditionally because I knew that there was and is something special about these men and women. I knew that these were God's children and I needed to move in excellence and virtue. Most of my time and energy was centered around the inmates and prison, so God had to allow these major shifts in my life to catapult me into my next. My next season of mothering, mentoring, leadership and walking fully in my Apostolic calling. God told me that I was called to the nations and what he required of me was heavy.

SPOKEN WORD

Title: It's On The Other Side

It's on the other side, you will be satisfied
Filled up, over the top, on the overflowing side
You will arise, in a ride, on overdrive
When you arrive, tell them you derived, from the other side
I'm not going to lie, you're not going to believe your eyes
You're going to have to blink, and pinch yourself a 1000 times
You're going to know its real, it's happening in real times
They don't never have to ask How your doing?
Your looking real fine!
Now You're realizing and understanding
How the other side
Suppose to be close to you, as family members on your mother's
side
You can just relax and chill on the other side
I could of been traumatized, but I got open eyes
I use to be all about that bread (meaning money)
I couldn't see another side
I could of been dead a couple times
Left with a big whole inside, on the bagel side
I had a void , I was empty, I'm still learning why
I had to cross a river of pain, now I remain on the other side
        You will find peace on the other side
After you say peace to the other side
Just like cooking meat, when its getting fried
Sooner or later, your going to have to flip to the other side
Inside I'm free like the other side
Like a barber, I compare this side to the other side
Even if its mines, it get shared, like a side of fries
I was on the side line, still looking at the other side

They was all surprised, like, "How you get here from the other side"
Every door opened up I could of came in through the side
Never will I be stressed and depressed, rolling my eyes
My mind is free, and not confined
I can't get caught up like them other guys
I pray that everything be parallel and stay straight
If you don't hear me, you going to feel me eventually, I'm on vibrate
It's like I could see better when I close my eyes
I know I'm here, but my thoughts, somewhere on the other side
My imagination, takes me places, I don't need to drive
They say " the mind is a terribly thing to waste" I recycle mines
I use what I learned , again and again, on the other side
If your still reading you already agreed its on the other side!
It's on the other side, you will be satisfied
Filled up , over the top, on the overflowing side

Written By
Charles – CW

CHAPTER THIRTEEN

PREPARING FOR A BIGGER HARVEST

HEART BREAK AND BETRAYAL are two of the deadliest things: they both can do some serious damage to your soul and spirit if you allow those emotions and feelings to overtake you. I was in a dark place in my life, but I was not ready to give up and quit. I refused to believe that my ministry was over. God did not bring me this far for me to just roll over and die. So, in spite of what the enemy was trying to whisper in my ear, I knew I had to keep my focus on Jesus. Most of the time when God is doing some major shifting in your life, you can't see the light at the end of the tunnel right way. You just have to have faith that He is going to guide you through it.

As I sought the Lord and asked him why I was feeling abandoned, rejected and now visionless; what am I to do? The Lord spoke softly, and He told me that he wanted me to help hurting women. The Lord told me that there are many powerful women who have been sitting, misused, abused, and even overlooked. The Lord spoke to my spirit and told me that my hurts and pains were not just from the prison but also from my past. I knew then as a leader, as a woman called by God, that if I was to ever be free, if I was to ever walk in total healing and wholeness, I was going to have to revisit my past and I was going to have to dig deep and get to the root of my heart issues.

This is when the Lord spoke to me about my second book, *An Unveiled Heart*, where I released all of my past hurts, and guiding women through the process of healing. God had begun to take the broken pieces of my heart and he was slowly mending them back together. In addition, I had a few allies in the administrative office whom I would talk to from time to time and they really helped me to recover just by listening, understanding and speaking on my behalf. So, as I began to write, I was getting free from all the stuff that had me bound. My joy was returning, and I could see a path in that tunnel that looked so dark and gloomy. Once *An Unveiled Heart* was listed on Amazon, I scheduled book signings and did conferences where women, and men, came, and the Holy Spirit moved just like he did those years when I was laboring in the prison. The time I spent going into the dark world of prison all those years prepared me to shine that same light. That light of hope and healing, that light of love and commitment. That light of transition and change, that light of wholeness and empowerment, inspiring not just men and women behind physical bars, but the men and women who are in caged within their minds.

I now have full understanding that God has called me to continue to set the captives free to a harvest that He has already prepared. I thank the Lord for keeping me and allowing me to go through all the hurts the pains and the losses. Only God can turn your pain into passion, your misery into your ministry and your dark places into a breaking of the day! Today, I'm ok with being known as a strong black woman, a queen, a woman who many say is the total package. I'm confident, and I love God, I know that I possess an inner strength that most women don't have and I'm ok with not being most women. I had to learn that my journey is my journey and I appreciate the path that God has taken me on. It was my journey through the prisons, and all the experiences, that built who I am today. The Lord let me know that he was resetting some things in my life so he could send me to a bigger harvest; he was hitting the rest button. God told me that my labor was not in vain and for those who sat under my tutelage in the prison, that a harvest had been birth and they are now equipped to carry the torch! These men are still standing and moving in the Holy Spirit still impacting lives. This is what the Holy Spirit revealed to me when I was writing my book, *An Unveiled Heart.*

Looking back over my life, I always thought that there were no do-overs. This is true in some things, but God can and is a God of second chances. I understand with the realization that I can't go back and change the past no matter how difficult and shameful it was. What I hold valuable today is that I am ok with the old chapters being closed in my life because they cannot be rewritten; and to be honest with you, some books need to stay closed. I can now start to write new chapters in my life that empower, encourage, and recharge those who he sends me to because I was able to own up to the events in my life that have shaped, molded, and made me into the woman I am today.

I heard my virtual coach say it like this, and I'm going to paraphrase it: *You made your past decisions on the information you had then, now you can make your future decisions based on the information you have now.* This means I am not going to live in regret about my process or the length of it. The fact of the matter is that with the information I have now and walking with an unveiled heart, I can hit the reset button and turn the pages of the new and exciting chapters of my life. This does not mean that everything will be unicorns and rainbows. It just simply means that I have a new perspective on what God is doing in my life, and my faith is increased, knowing that all things are working for my good. When I think about the word reset, it means **to set again or anew, to readjust, to change and to restore. It means the act or an instance of setting again (Webster's Dictionary).**

When I began to walk down my road to true healing, with the grace of God to hit the reset button of my life, I had to own up to the things that have happened in my life and deal with the pain and the reality of all the disappointments and setbacks, and then I had to let it go. When you reset your life, you have to be able let go of the past so you can embrace the present and make room for the future. After almost 32 years of building me, the Lord has now allowed me to share my process openly, but the key to the whole thing was I had to be ok with being transparent about my journey.

I had to be ok with reopening those doors and allowing myself to feel everything all over again because I wanted to make sure that I was totally healed. I want you to understand that if he did it for me, then surely, he will do it or you! In my book, *While You Wait*, I discuss a season in my life where God introduced me to my current husband, Frank, whom I love and honor very much. In Chapter 10 of that book, the title talks about the process of loving me. Check it out! The first step in loving me was figuring out who I was. What did I like? What made me tick? What were my desires?

What was my personal style? Once I figured out who I was, it was time to implement the plan. I started small and worked my way up to the big goals. And when I reached a small goal, I'd celebrate myself. I would keep this process up until I felt confident in who I was created to be. It was time for no more excuses! First things first! My friend Delisa who puts it this way, "We make time for what we deem as important in our lives and for everything else we make excuses." This meant getting over all my woes, making my list, and checking it twice in search of the real me.

When people look at me now, they see this confident woman who knows what she wants and lets nothing, or no one, get in her way; a girl who plays big and walks unapologetically. But to tell the truth, I was not born with courage oozing out of my fingertips. I did not always walk with my head up high. When I looked in the mirror, I did not always like what I saw.

As a matter of fact, I used to run from the mirror or anything I thought was a challenge to grow. It was God who helped me to recreate myself, teaching me about purpose, destiny, and how to just BE! I also had a belief that all things are possible. I was that girl on welfare who dropped out of school because of tragedy. I was that young girl raising three children before the age of twenty-one. I was that girl who was mentally, physically, emotionally, and sexually abused. I was that girl who thought she found her escape in drugs and drinking. I was that girl who searched for love in all the wrong places and made all the wrong choices.

I was that girl that life had seemingly kicked to the curb and said, "Do not pass go!" I was that girl who was told that I was never going to make it or be anything. I was her, that girl without a house or home. I did not get free from the bondage of life until I made a choice to give my life to Christ, and he started pouring life into me, delivering me from myself, people, and my past hurts. I have learned that to move forward, you must leave the past behind you. There is hope and peace around the corner in the next chapter of your life. All you have to do is take a step forward. There were times that I felt alone. There were times when I felt scared, but the same way God kept me, he will keep you while on your journey.

Men and Ladies, it's your pain that births your passion; your misery will turn into and become your ministry. Your hurts can be the catalyst for your healing and others. All things can and do work together for good in your life. **Romans 8:28 states, "And we know that all things work together for good to them that love God, to them who are the called according to his purpose."** So, that lets me know that no matter what you are going through right now in your life, it is working out for good in the long run.

You will gain more wisdom, more understanding, and a little patience, but most of all, you will learn how to put your trust and faith in God, which will see you through no matter what. As you can see, I give God all the Glory because I know that I would not be here today if He had not shown His hand like He did so many times in my life. So, ladies and gentlemen I urge you to take another look in the mirror, and this time see yourself like God sees you.

Psalms 139:14 says, "I will praise thee; for I am fearfully and wonderfully made: marvelous are thy works; and that my soul knoweth right well. This tells me you are made of the good stuff! In the scriptures, God calls you the apple of his eye. Look at what he says in **Deuteronomy 32:10: "He found him in a desert land, in a barren, howling wilderness; He surrounded him, He instructed him, He guarded him as the apple of His eye."**

Psalm 17:8," Keep me as the apple of your eye; hide me in the shadow of Your wings."
Proverbs 7:2," Keep my commandments and live; guard my teachings as the apple of your eye."

You have an inner and outer strength that is without measure. You were fashioned and formed in his likeness. You were made to be creative, witty, and energetic. You are Kings and Queens, and you were made to rule and reign! You have everything you need, so now is the time for you to reset your life. It's time for you to move in motion the things pertaining to your vision and your purpose. Yes, my brothers and sisters, you have a purpose, but God is going to stir up your passion that will drive that purpose that will help you reach your destiny.

My brothers and sisters, I want to encourage you to rewind, reset, rediscover, and recalibrate your life, allowing God to restore the confidence that has been lost over the years so you can revive the real you! After my journey in darkness and many sessions of rewinding the tape and restructuring my life, God has continued to bless me. You see, going into the prisons all those years was my game changer; It was my process of building and making. Today, I am still moving forward alongside a loving and caring husband who lifts me up, builds me, honors me, and he encourages me, pushing me with the Godly love I need as I continue my exciting journey in God. And for the record, I AM HEALED!! I have no ill feelings and I know what happened, was supposed to happen, the way it happened. Today I can say that with a pure and healed heart. I know that this was for my learning and my maturing.

Brothers and sisters, resetting your life will allow you to go back and obtain the things you thought were never possible. It will allow you to dream again, live again, and love again. To those men and women who allowed me to pour into their lives, remember what you have been taught, continue to let your light shine, and build from the inside out! Remember, rewind, rediscover, reset, and recalibrate to be restored!

You are the true Sons of Thunder, and I am so honored that God allowed me to impart, mentor, teach, train, and for some, be a spiritual mother in the Lord and a lifelong friend. Until our paths cross again, be at peace and know that I look forward to seeing you on the other side of the gate!

As we use to say in The Family Is First Project,

HERE WE COME!

IN HONOR OF THE FAMILIES, THE TEAM, AND MEN OF THE FAMILY IS FIRST PROJECT

Family is one of the most important, if not the most important thing in our lives. Taking time every day to appreciate your loved ones for all that they do helps us to reconnect, strengthen, and grow as a family. We will forever be FAMILY!

"The memories we make with our family is everything." —Quote By Candace Cameron Bure

CHAPTER FOURTEEN

THE SONS OF THUNDER ON THE OUTSIDE

I WAS INCARCERATED FOR 22 YEARS of my life; prison affected me emotionally by placing me in a mindset of survival of the fittest. While in prison I was affected spiritually. I was stripped of all self-sufficiency where I had to seek God and Him alone. It also affected me socially where I sought to be connected with men who had the same purpose and vision for their lives. The event that started my transformation process was losing everything; I came to a place in my life where I was headed for destruction. I led a lifestyle of destruction and despair that landed me in prison.

It seemed like God had closed every door in my life; while in prison, I did not receive any letters from my family, or visits. This threw me into a place of seeking and figuring out what my real purpose was. I knew this was not my end and this was not going to be my destiny. I felt that there has to be something better than a life behind prison bars and adopting this mindset started my transformation process. Prison is where I found God, this was my divine encounter. Prison is where I met God face to face and my whole life changed. Before my incarceration, I was on the run from parole; I decided to turn myself in. One evening I was laying in my cell waiting to be processed, reflecting on my life of crime, drugs, and pain. I looked at my life and the revolving door of prison stays. My birthday was soon approaching. I remember calling my mother and telling her if you bring me a bible then I will change my life. My mother sent a bible to the prison on my birthday; once I received that bible, I would read the word every day, and sometimes I will fall asleep with that bible lying on my chest.

Every day I felt the Lord drawing me closer to Him; this is when I took off. I began pursuing God and as I pursued God, he pursued me. My spirit was awakened, and this was my divine encounter. I look at my transformation in God as my true success, having a true conversion allowed me to stand as a man who was coming into his purpose. This allowed me to reach other inmates through teaching and preaching the Word of God in my cell or block. This placed me in a position to reach men from a different perspective who were opposed to how I used to reach them when I was in the streets talking with all the slang; you know, the language from the streets.

I now had a new walk and a new talk and this time I could tell of the goodness of God and how he transformed me. The men in prison started to become enlightened and they started seeing and hearing something special they never saw from an inmate before. I would reach the men through prayer, fellowship and reading the word of God to them. We would gather in the halls and have some honest and deep conversations about our previous lives and how God was transforming us to be greater than we could ever be. This was something new that the inmates had never had before. Preaching and teaching in the cell block, talking about God, building relationships. My words of encouragement to you: Try something that you never tried before; get away from everybody and everything and get to a place where God can strip you totally from all self-sufficiency that you have no choice but to lean on him. He will start to speak to you and awaken your spirit; he will start to show you things, and this is what helped me, and he will help you. When I think of being a son of thunder, I think of power and authority to rule over my life.

With Respect and Love,
Apostle Frank J. Johnson Jr

***

Well, where do I begin? I remember our very first assignment was to write a paper, however long, about yourself, your background, where you come from, what got you here and what your aspirations are for the future. I've always been a better writer than speaker. I think my homework was a few pages long, but I could have gone longer. Prison gives you time to reflect. I did just that, as I was able to share with Apostle Stacie exactly who I was and why I ended up in this situation.

I was pleased with that. In order for someone to really connect with you, I believe it's important for them to profoundly observe and get to know you. I felt that was her genuine purpose. I knew prison wasn't my destiny. It was a pit stop for me to rotate my tires, change my oil, and upgrade my mindset. I took advantage of that. The Family Is First Project was a different kind of program. It wasn't for good days, it wasn't for a judicial release; it had no hidden agenda, and you couldn't fake it. We became a family, a unit. As a woman, Apostle Stacie was able to lead and direct us into connecting with our families on the outside in a deeper way than just visits to eat snacks and ramble on. More than just jail calls about "What you doing, and did you do that for me yet?"

For a woman in a prison setting, surrounded by all men, this was no easy task. She held her own, and when she opened her mouth to speak, you knew she was no joke. Her husband knew she was fit for that role. I can't say I could send my woman in there like that, it takes a lot. Their relationship spoke volumes and they set a great example. Her husband did 20 years and she stood by him for 10 of those years. She could relate!!! It is vital to understand what our family goes through as well for them to understand us. It's hard for our family members to ride that out with us. We have to be aware of that and not take advantage of them and not drain them. They have a lot going on out there in the world where bills are due, kids are exigent, and they have goals as well as aspirations of their own. I was able to bond with my family in a much better way through the lens Apostle Stacie gave us.

We were forced to talk about things that were important, with each other in group and with our family members. This was everything we needed, building on the good and destroying the bad and miscellaneous. She met my mother; they became friends to this day. Apostle Stacie and I are friends to this day. We can talk about whatever; she relates. She calls me her other son. I love Apostle Stacie. She can get on stage, preach, and rock a crowd just as good as Tupac lol. You will be intrigued. I remember she passed around this book to all of us inmates in group one day. It was a short read, called "Conversations on Manhood." It was a great read. It helped me develop a grown man's mindset and transition out of the boy I was when I came to prison.

The guy who wrote it had done a long time in prison. She got him to come talk to us one day, and he was enlightening. One of the most important things I got out of that book was, "The use of profanity is a feeble mind forcibly trying to explain itself because it has no other way of expressing its meaning," that stuck with me. So basically, we curse because we are lazy minded. We are not growing and expanding our vocabulary and our vision. I've never thought about how ignorant cursing sounds before then. Don't get it twisted; I'm from Lincoln Heights, Cincinnati. My young teenage years were wild and ruthless. I was crazy, violent, and retarded just like some of you, or worse. But I've been HEALING and GROWING for a long time. I refuse to be stuck with who I used to be, and the demons I still face. We have to live in our reality, and let the truth guide, not shame us.

I have family members, "brothers" and cousins still doing time, some are never coming home. I love them DEARLY. I don't want to be a thug forever. I don't want to be ignorant. I like the finer things in life. I like boujie and classy females, not ratchet ones. I love the idea of me being who I am. A Black man with a hood background that can wear Nike joggers daily but also switch up into a suit and tie or Mauvais formal attire and conduct a business meeting with the white man. I like to smell good. I don't want to be high every single day. I don't want to die in Ohio. I love women; I love life. I want to travel the world. I want more than the average dope boy who aspires to have six figures. I'm a 10-figure ni***. Straight up. So, I have to walk and talk in that way. It's not cool to be stupid. What do you want to teach your children? What do you want them to be? What do you want from life!?This is the most important question and answer that I pondered.

What do I want from life? Not just what you want to be, but what do you want life to offer you, in every aspect. After sitting in confinement for 5 years, plus the years beforehand, when I was "free" but in the prison of my own mind, I learned I need freedom. I have to have it, the freedom to come and go as I please. Financial freedom, freedom of the mind and not just a one tracked naive mindset. The freedom to be with my children, wife, family and travel the world without being enslaved to an employer. Health is freedom, to live long. Knowledge is freedom. When you know better, you do better, and you stay out of situations you only wish you could go back and change.

Freedom is everything to me. Don't contradict yourself and say you want peace, but you cause hell to some people. Don't contradict yourself in saying you want to be free, but you run the streets every day. Align yourself with what you want, live in integrity and honesty. You are in control of your destiny, go get what you want. Every adversity is a blessing, only if you can train your mind to see that it can seed the outcome of something equal in benefits to you. Apostle Frank, Apostle Stacie's husband, also came out and spoke with us one day at the program.

He was a buff guy, he had on good cologne, and the latest fashion of designer clothes on at the time. "He looked like money," we follow these things in America, and immediately he had my attention. But when he spoke, it was powerful. The most important thing he said was, "Don't spend all your time at the pull up and dip bar. Just as you want to strengthen your muscles to look and feel better, it is 100x more important to strengthen the muscles of the brain. Just as any other muscle, if you don't exercise it, it will get weak."

Life is too serious to have a weak brain. Our minds are fragile, think about the brain: it looks like it's made of noodle, and it's surrounded by our thick skull to protect it. It is fragile, that's why you see women and men selling their souls daily, because life has eaten them up. This is something I will never succumb to. My name means too much to me. I am a very busy guy now a days, but when Apostle Stacie called for this slight favor, I couldn't help but pause for a second to do what I could for her.

I know she'd do the same for me and has. That is what it's about. Building relationships and helping each other succeed. Don't become a product of your environment. Self-education is the most important education. The saying goes, if you want to hide something from a ni***, put it in a book. True statement. We don't read! I never have before prison. I've been reading ever since The Family Is First Project. That has literally saved me. I have been home from prison for 2 1/2 years and I continue to read, work out, listen to audible books, reflect, educate myself and progress deliberately. Growth and evolution are life's necessities. Don't get left behind. Whatever is not growing is dying. You can't stay the same. I'm happy to get the opportunity to connect with you. This is only the very beginning. Live in reality, take advantage of your journey, aim high, be relentless, be fearless, be patient, be discipline. You will make it. We will connect again.

Always Peace,
Nick R

* * *

Hello reader, my name is William. I was born on the west side and raised uptown in the city of Cincinnati. I would like to share with you how The Family Is First Project and Adonai Ministries has impacted my life. Yes, my life. At the age of 24, I was sentenced to 5 years in prison. Since it was my first time in prison, I didn't know what to expect but I knew I was going to need some kind of guidance to get through my sentence.

Once incarcerated I quickly realized I needed to change my life and I didn't want to get involved with the nonsense that was going on in prison. I started signing up for different programs so that I can stay busy, but I really wasn't learning anything. I seen a post for Adonai Ministries "The Family Is First Project" and signed up. The first day I heard Apostle Stacie's voice, I knew I was supposed to be there. Her voice was powerful, clear, and meaningful. She told us, a group of both young and older men, that "play time was over with." At that time, I was in the building stages of a relationship. She taught me how not to add extra weight/stress to my loved ones. I learned how to communicate and to be more understanding. The Family is First Project has helped me grow and realize my role as a leader. Adonai Ministries' amazing team has had a huge impact on my life. Even after being released from prison, they are still here like family when I need them. The Family Is First Project is for real!

Forever grateful,
William J

* * *

It's my honor to submit this brief information about The Family is First Project: Allow me to start by stating that I was incarcerated for a total prison time of Ten Years. I had completed a Seven Year straight sentence when I first encountered The Family is First Project. Prison had its impact. Some positive - Some negative. First, my negative impacts were, and I must say, the most significant and traumatic: It was the fact that I was separated from my Three (3) year old son (at the time of my departure).

Secondly, being taken from society and all of its normal environments and placed in an environment that harbored "abnormalities" were devastating and emotionally traumatic. Spiritually, my faith was challenged. I had reduced to doubting if my life was ever to find purpose. After so many attempts at success yet hindered by so many failures. I got to the point of believing that this was my last attempt. Socially, my relationships with my parents and friends had suffered. This provided a wedge between us due to all of my lies, inability to follow-through, and inconsistencies.

The Family is First Project was significant in providing tools necessary for spiritual growth. It not only demonstrated from a practical standpoint, but also walked the participants through at a pace where it was easy to understand. I was moved with HOPE by personal testimonies. Speakers who shared their experiences of surviving after incarcerations, addictions, and abuses.

The fact that they were able to mend broken relationships with wives, kids, employers, etc., deposited a healthy and new essence of HOPE. I then, too, believed God would do that for me. After my incarceration, I went on to become a self-published, White House- recognized Author, Inspirational Speaker, and Youth Intervention Specialist, and more. I've been able to secure financial contracts with agencies in our community where I had once been in treatment. To date, I've created my own Profit Youth Organization and Non-Profit Organization. Through the practical principles and structure of The Family is First Project, I was able to continue to build upon my release from the foundation that was giving to me while incarcerated. It is through meaningful, heartfelt, and purposeful programs such as The Family is First Project, that society and families can be healed and restored.

Conclusion:

For anyone reading my brief narrative, my hopes would be that you first know and believe that "God has a greater plan for your LIFE!" Your experiences are all working for your good and God's glory! I know it doesn't feel good - but endure the refining process. You are the diamond that God has chosen. Whether you are just starting your journey or, has been on the path for quite some time - God's timetable does NOT work on the same timeline as ours.

The one thing I've learned from all of my many years of ups, downs, failures, loss of faith, and addictions - to my restoration and ability to now walk in God's plan for my life, is that, although I went astray countless times God stayed FAITHFUL! HOPE is all we have, my brothers and sisters. Hold fast at all costs. The day will come that, just as I am now receiving the everlasting hand of God's Mercies and Grace upon my life - the same would be of YOU - if . . . you stay the course!

De'Ron Smith

Author, Intervention Specialist, Inspirational Speaker

* * *

I thank God for Apostle Stacie! During a very difficult time in my life. She came like a ray of sun shining through a dark cloud. I was back in prison for a parole violation. I blamed the system, but Apostle Stacie showed me where I needed to be accountable as well. I had gone home after serving an 18 to life sentence but I wasn't in shape to remain free. My priorities needed to be rearranged. I needed to put family first! Apostle Stacie would begin every class with a Hearty Prayer; it was like mini-Church. She wouldn't allow any spirits of negativity to invade our sessions. She would make phone calls to my children's mother to give her progress reports on me. I learned from a Woman just how it feels to be alone on the other side of the fence, "Waiting on a phone call".

I learned the need to have healthy boundaries in a relationship. Above all, Apostle Stacie taught me to Trust God, even when it appears the situation will not change. I am now free again, spending valuable time with my 6-year-old daughter and my 8-year-old son. I thank God for giving you the courage to walk into a men's facility by yourself with the mission on your mind, Apostle Stacie. I pray that you continue to be blessed in every way. Truly your brother,

Kevin Coleman

* * *

I was incarcerated for six years from May 2015 – March 2021 at NCCI, I like to explain to people that, before prison, I thought I was the top dog in the world. I was a military officer, making over $100,000 a year. I had money, power, status, material things. Everything you would think would make you happy. I didn't think I needed anyone – especially not God. People needed me, not the other way around. However, God showed me how wrong I was. I was dead on the inside, and if He didn't slow me down by sitting my butt in prison, I would be dead on the outside too!

I came to prison broken physically, mentally, and spiritually. God ripped my figurative clothes from me until I was naked in front of Him. My clothes were my status, money, sins, comforts, etc. I went from the top to the bottom in a massive fall (Proverbs 16:18). God didn't say a word; He just stared at me. It was awkward and uncomfortable.

Until – it wasn't. I realized at that moment that nakedness was exactly how God wanted me. Just as Adam & Eve were naked and shameless in front of God (Genesis 2:25), so was I. Jesus Christ was the cornerstone in the new foundation that God was building in me. A part of the growth came in the form of the Family is First Project. It was different than any program I had seen before. It was not just a "check the box" type of program where the staff person was just getting through it and moving on. Apostle Stacie cared about our families and us. It was great to see. I was privileged enough to facilitate the class alongside Apostle Stacie.

Men were reluctant and apprehensive at the beginning. Regardless, after they saw that Apostle Stacie was real, they opened up very quickly. I got to see men change before my eyes. Even non-Christian men's hearts were being softened (Ezekiel 36:26). It was amazing to watch families come together. Some men haven't had contact with their families in years. The tears flowed abundantly.

I know that Family is First Project changed men and impacted people's lives: inmates, family, and staff alike. The program gave me confidence and boldness to go out and follow where God was leading me. I have been a part of many small groups and Bible studies in prison. I know that God moved people through me by being a willing vessel. I am a better person for going through the program. If you are reading this in prison and feeling hopeless and helpless, remember one thing: God loves you no matter what. And He will use you anywhere you are.

He placed you in this exact spot for a reason. Don't allow this world to jade you and turn your heart into stone. God is always at work around you and inviting you to join Him in that work. Just look for where He is. If you keep moving in the direction God has for you, you will see fruit. God sent us out to make disciples. He didn't say it would be in a place you would want to be in! Keep the faith!

Josh Ewing

* * *

My name is Jeffery Carson I served 5 1/2 years on a 10yr. sentence. During the latter part of my third year going into my fourth year of incarceration. I was privileged to go through the Family First Is First Project taught and facilitated by none other than Mrs. Stacie Johnson herself. I had been hearing from other men in the prison, who previously had graduated how great the program was. They all recommended I take it. I am so glad I did! In most cases one would only stand to reason how much a woman's perspective would benefit a group of all men, in prison. I gain so much insight and understanding to the reality of my wife and loved ones. It gave a safe place, tools, and encouragement for my family and how to open up and share about the truth of what life looks and feels likes for us on a day-to-day basis. We discovered how much we can trust one another with the truth. We learned how important honesty, and transparency is. Through Mrs. Stacie Johnson personal testimony, passion, and level of transparency.

It put words to my wife's and family members feelings and experiences that they could not express just yet being that they were still in it. Mrs. Stacie Johnson insight, information, class sessions, and homework assignments brought me and my family to a higher level of empathy, compassion, love, and understanding that no other program was able to. Apostle Stacie asked a question at the beginning of one of our classes. How do you find or be normal in an abnormal situation? Well, The Family Is First Project with the tools and information and the amazing facilitation skills of Apostle Stacie helped us answer that question. You see The Family Is First Project brought some normalcy to my family and my abnormal situation. We are ever so grateful and appreciative to Mrs. Stacie Johnson and The Family Is First Project. Today, my family and I still use the information and reflect on our growth moments we had throughout the class sessions in prison.

Thank you, Mrs. Stacie Johnson and The Family Is First Project.
Sincerely Jeffery and Shalana Carson,
The Carson Family

* * *

Hi, I am Qa'id Salaam. I served 13 years in prison. While being incarcerated I stumbled upon a newly offered program at WCI that was geared towards family values I heard. So, after the first year of it being ran at the prison, I gathered a lot of great feedback from the participants, and I decided to join. Not know that it would be of great help in the long run. I along with my mother and father joined the Family is First Project with open minds. We gained so much understanding, we broke long standing frustration over opposite sides of communication and how I learned a great listener is an even better talker. Because you learn how to use the right words to express the right emotions that you are feeling.

My father and I really had that type of barrier to destroy. And we did! My mother and I also had the opportunity to join the alumni panel, and in doing so we helped others gain clarity in their own relationships with family, girlfriends, boyfriends, mothers, fathers etc… This helped me stay focused on getting my life sentence overturned. In which I later did in 2020. You never know what guidance you need until obstacles are in your face. But I can tell you from experience this is one that can change your thoughts for the better. And if you plan on joining this one of a lifetime program. I ask that you come with an open mind and open ears to learn how to inspire those around you by learning how to express your words in a meaningful way. Thank you, The Family is First Project for all you have done for me and others in this struggle of misunderstandings.

Sincerely,
Qa'id Salaam

"Coming together is a beginning, staying together is progress, and working together is success." – Henry Ford

CHAPTER FIFTEEN

WORDS FROM THE TEAM

I TRULY LOVED being a part of the Family is First Project. From seeing all the men changed their lives, to the teaching and sermons on Sunday mornings. There were two men that made an impact on me as I volunteered with the program. One of those men was only 19 years old and facing life the other young man was a father who had 8 children and he was also facing life. When we first met them, they were so angry and really did not trust people at all. Because they had found themselves in a position that they had no control over.

They signed up for the Family is First Project and did the easy part: the book work that was accepted in the class. I remember they would come and sit down and neither of them would say anything. But I could tell that they were listening, hearing about God and His plan for their lives. Then one day out of the blue they walked in the room with big smiles on their faces and began to participate and really be a part of the class. They started to attend service on Sundays when Apostle Stacie had to preach and participating in the service activities. It really blessed me to see how these men blossomed in the Family is First Project and this made it worth all the early morning trips up and down the highway.

I also remember the Family Days; this was a time when the prison allowed the families to come and have class with the men on a day that was not assigned for regular visitation. I was so blessed to watch both families and inmate gain an understanding of what they were feeling and how they could deal with their present situation. And not to mention the blessed celebration. Apostle Stacie would have a graduation ceremony, celebrating all of the men for all of the hard work that they did to complete the program, and believe me Apostle Stacie did not make it easy. If the men made it to the celebration, Apostle Stacie made sure that they were fully equipped and ready!

I truly have a different idea of men behind bars now. I learned that some of those men just made some bad choices, but they were good people. The Family Is First Project helped the inmates and families both to deal with their present decisions and how to forgive themselves. In addition, they learn to trust God right where they are.

I'm so grateful for the opportunity to have been a part of this phenomenal experience and I do pray for this program to one day start again. Thank you, Apostle Stacie Johnson for the opportunity to be a part, there are more roads to travel spreading The Families is First project to the nations.

With dearest love,
Evangelist Loretta Phillips

* * *

While some prisons and penitentiaries make you feel a bit on the edge, the experiences are very real. Men and women are being locked up each and every day somewhere around the country. My experiences have been over 25 plus years visiting other inmates. Each and every inmate experiences are different and quite unique. Each crime happened a different way, place, and time period, but still they all arrived at the same places, nevertheless. I've been in and out of many prisons throughout the Ohio area for visits. Seeing the many faces, ethnicities, cultures, sizes of both men and women alike incarcerated behind bars. Before going into the prison system, each time, we start off with a word of prayer to cover us in the name of Jesus and his blood.

We are checked in with sometimes a chaplain of the prison to give us escort through the place for services to take place. Then all the inmates that want to come to the services will start coming in to take a seat and get themselves position and ready for services.

Many come for various reason, to pass away time, get a different view of the ones coming, enjoy the Lord, and experience something brand new for those that have never attended a prison service for the very first time. Most times we start off in the services with a greeting to all the inmates trying to make them feel welcomed and at home.

The services take off from there with reading the Word of GOD and singing some praise and worship songs to invite the Lord into the services. Then the most important part of the services takes place: THE WORD OF GOD. The place gets very quiet, and all ears and eyes are listening and seeing. The altar call is rendered, or given, and the souls start coming down to the front for giving their lives to the Lord for the very first time as they know it; tears flow, everyone has a different reaction to GOD'S word when it is heard. My role with The Family Is First Project was to be a prayer warrior and that is to pray and watch for the attacks of the enemy spiritually. I've served with Adonai Ministries 5-7 years approximately... we visited many prisons throughout Ohio.

The Family Is First Project let me get a firsthand insight on others that wanted to change to do better and be better, realizing the shift in their lives that have taken place. One of my greatest memories was seeing a change in others as they accepted Christ into their lives. There were also some challenges. I remember one time I was the only person who went with Apostle Stacie to the prison.

It was just us two and I was delegated to do the opening prayer and the greetings, while watching as her armor bearer, all at the same time; but God moved in a mighty way and things turned out fine. Thank you, Apostle Stacie, for allowing me to experience God in a way that can never be matched!

Grace and peace with many blessings,
  Pastor Carl Burden

* * *

I was a part of Apostle Stacie's ministry team. I went into the prison for the first time not knowing what to expect. I was not prepared fully to go into a system that shut up everything behind you such as how the doors slammed and you were locked in; but yet, you have to keep walking to move forward. I remember seeing all these Black men young enough to be my children and wondering to myself what happened? Why? Who dropped the ball? It did not take long for me to look at them and not see the things they had done, being dressed in their prison clothes, but seeing them as young men, babies like my babies. My heart went out to them, and I wept internally.

These men were all shapes, colors, and sizes. Color didn't matter. They were and are people. Yet, for or by the grace of God, I understood that it could have been me in a system labeled and locked down. So, when I went in, I knew there was no physical touch, so my heart hugged everyone.

Because of that, they called me Momma Cheryl. My heart seen the truth, great and small. It sees people's life emotions. Just like God sees us, I saw them through the eyes of a mother. My babies....... The experience was amazing and sometimes too overwhelming, yet I was well received and willing to be there for them. I remember walking through gates and yards for the worship experience just to hear songs from the heart sung by these inmates. Testimonies and cries from their broken past. I saw real life, real people, and real men and women who were taught real talk from Apostle Stacie and her team. These men and women were being healed and learning to walk in total forgiveness. My role was a minister worker as a helper to the ministry and Apostle Stacie, for 2yrs plus.

The family was to be first always. Adonai Ministries took that saying to another level understanding the pains and traumas of being away from home and returning back to home. Apostle Stacie taught us that these men and women were not left and not forgotten. The Family Is First Project and Adonai Ministries made it up close and personal. My greatest memory is seeing people who had made mistakes and who were wounded were still desiring that much needed attention and love from someone who cared. Just as the inmates saw hope, Apostle Stacie and her team of leaders saw hope in the hearts of the men and women, they had a press for life in spite of the prison challenges.

Praise God.
Pastor Cheryl Burden
AKA Mama Cheryl

* * *

I would like to say thank you Adonai Ministries for the opportunity to be a part to the ministerial team that worked alongside of the ministries within Ohio penitentiaries. To see firsthand how The Family Is First Project were uniting men and women who were incarcerated to their love ones outside the prisons in order to restore those families before the inmates transitioned back into our communities, this blessed our hearts tremendously. Fruit of the Harvest Ministries was so honored to witness such mighty moves of God because of your years of commitment to the work.

We love you, Pastor Chris and Apostle Chantell Robinson

* * *

For three years, I walked alongside Apostle Stacie Johnson and The Family Is First Program (TFFP). I had never been inside a prison until I joined Apostle Stacie. Having an active imagination, I envisioned all sorts of things happening to us (like prison riots) before I even walked through the door. What I found was a group of men who, for varying reasons, found themselves locked into a system they couldn't escape from. When I entered the prison, these men were inmates, criminals. When I left, they were sons, brothers, husbands and fathers.

During my time with the program, I witnessed Apostle Stacie reach areas in the men's' hearts, souls and minds that others were unable to reach. I witnessed the walls barring communication between the men and their family members begin to crumble. I witnessed fathers hug their sons for the first time in years. I witnessed sons, husbands and fathers apologize for the first time for their part in the near desolation of their family unit. I witnessed mothers, wives, girlfriends cry and pour out their pain and their frustrations in the safe place that the Family Is First Project provided. I witnessed Apostle Stacie administer tough love on the men as if she birthed them herself.

She was tough when needed but always compassionate. She didn't view them as inmates. She viewed them as the sons of God they were. When others counted them out, Apostle Stacie counted them in and helped to build them back up through biblical teachings. She was tough, straightforward, and forthright. She preached from the Word and from her experiences as a prison wife.

I witnessed family members breathe a sigh of relief when Apostle Stacie shared her story as a prison wife. I witnessed shock on the men's faces once they learned Apostle Stacie married an inmate. To both groups, Apostle Stacie could relate, and that bit of knowledge helped the participants of the program to relax enough to tell their own stories. That bit of knowledge allowed the men to soften up enough to allow a woman, who they at first thought could not do anything for them, to minister to them and to their situations. She made the men, and the families, take accountability for their own actions, and in so doing, relationships were renewed, strengthened, and have since endured.

The men and families worked hard to heal the broken places in their relationships with one another. They attended mandatory classes and did the homework that was designed to make each person look deep within themselves without the rose-colored glasses. And at the end of the program, the men and families that completed the program were celebrated, and that was my favorite part of the program. We celebrated the group with a party with each participant receiving their own certificate of completion from the ministry. We had food. We had cake. We had fun!
Love Always,
Minister April Jones

* * *

The Family First Project was a life changing blessing to me. It was truly a family. Under Apostle Stacie Johnson guidance and leadership, I learned how to communicate, I learned how to let go and allow healing and growth to happen. My very first time going into the prisons with Apostle Stacie, I cried like a baby. I had never been to a prison let alone in the inside behind the doors and bars. When I heard the doors slam shut behind us, I begin shaking from the inside out and I looked over and Apostle is walking in with so much authority, beauty, glow, poise, and integrity… I said let me pull it together and get into position. Listen, she educated, encouraged, taught, motivated; she fed them mind, body and spirit. Glory! I will never ever forget it. She actually saved me in the process and had no idea!!! I am blessed and honored to have been a part of the Family First Project.

Thank you, Apostle Stacie Johnson. Love you to life,
Evangelist Katina Phillips

* * *

Being a part of The Family is First Project is one of the most significant acts of kindness I have ever participated in! Matthew 25:36 reminds us to visit the incarcerated. The Family is First Project not only visits, but they teach, train, bridge the gap and celebrate the inmates and their families who are on the outside. I have never seen an effective program that teaches and counsels inmates and their families in preparation for the inmates return home. As the founder of TFFP, Stacie Johnson is a pioneer and passionate trendsetter who has never minded going behind bars to make a difference. To see the countenance of inmates uplifted because their accomplishments are being celebrated is something to behold. My favorite part of the program is the celebration, which speaks volumes about the impact of a truly transformational ministry!

His servant,
Pastor Delisa McIntosh

* * *

My experience with the Family Is First Project and Adonai ministries with Apostle Stacie Johnson began during late spring early summer of 2019. The impact of the Family is First Project can best be described as an awakening for me because it was my first time working with men in prison. The moment I stepped beyond the gates and was escorted to a room filled with prisoners, the faces that I saw seated in the room was very surprising.

The majority of these men were very young in age, which explains where many of our future husbands, doctors, attorneys, and presidents have been living. Unfortunately, this brought tears to my eyes every time I left to get in my car. The idea of those inmates being someone's son bothered me. A mother never foresees her child growing up one day to live a portion of their adulthood incarcerated by bad choices. I realized that these adult men were facing consequences related to behaviors that were threatening to society. There were no justifiable circumstances for many of these offenders; especially, after I learned through different conversations that some actions were reoccurrences, heartless and brutal. For some of these men, they internalized their convictions as a way to survive or protect themselves from others whom they felt was a threat to them. I am so glad that there is a God who loves us enough to look beyond our faults to see the needs (I Tim.1: 12-17). If a person would assess their behaviors honestly, whether they were good or bad, we could say that dysfunctions do exist in us all.

What matters most is the way we deal with them when they affect individuals related or nonrelated to us. The Family Is First Project brought hope that was desperately needed to strengthen and add the support missing during the separation of loved ones that are incarcerated. The resource of intervention provided a tough love without judgment on a weekly basis through intensive teaching and accountability of one's actions. Empowering men from the inside world of prison is a heavy burden to carry in an environment that is filled with pain, hurts, disappointments, rejection, and abandonment.

Need I say more? Except God can heal the broken hearted and His power can deliver people from strongholds that held them captive in areas of their life from a child into years as an adult. This point leads me to one last memory that still captures my heart. Apostle Stacie and the team organized her last class as a celebration to recognize the men who completed the sessions and all the class work from her training. We informed the family members of each inmate so they could arrange their time to come for support. She selected a few speakers to share about the class. There was one guy in particular who found the courage to stand before everyone to share a poem he wrote about his life and discovery.

There was a moment of vulnerability that you could sense that made him uncomfortable, but when I say the brother told the truth, his honesty brought him freedom. He spoke about an internal message that broke down barriers in his life that God was healing from the past. I am reminded by this testimony to pray for the harvest and transformation that the Adonai Ministries and The Family Is First Project will bring to men and their families this New Year.

With heartfelt love,
Minister Tonya Sneed

* * *

When I was invited to be à part of the Family Is First Project, I knew I was now connected to something special. It has helped me gain an understanding how the cycle of imprisonment not only affects the individual, but the entire family. Apostle Stacie Johnson has a heart for supporting families during their time of separation, financial challenges, and loneliness. The Family Is First Project is needed and necessary to help families weather through the storm. It is a blessing to help Apostle Stacie Johnson fulfill this purpose that God has assigned to her.

With much love,
Pastor Stephanie Dugar

* * *

The calling on my life was answered and confirmed, my footsteps were ordered. I joined New Covenant Church were
I was free indeed in the spirit (confirmation) I had always wanted to experience a Jail or prison ministry but never really knew how to start. I have experience in leadership, Ushering, and Intercessory in the spirit of the Lord and street ministry through my trials and tribulations in the Kingdom. I used to wonder why I was so different, I was always thankful to see a new morning, to encourage others to have patience and teaching them how to listen to God. I could feel sorrow, pain, and confusion when others were hurting and wandering into darkness.

Through my testimonies I wanted to help others and tell them about Jesus or ask them if they wanted prayer or needed to talk. I would listen and pray to God, asking the Holy Spirit to give me the right words to say. Yes, I am a cheerful person and a cheerful giver, with no attachments, trusting and believing in the Lord and smiling (Corinthians 9:7) walking away singing Jesus loves you and so do I. One Sunday morning I went to church, and we had guest speakers Apostle Stacie an Apostle Frank., service was on fire!! The Holy Spirit was flowing, and everyone was on one accord. Apostle Stacie was introduced as the founder of The Family Is First Project and Adonai Ministries, she needed help with the prison ministry she was doing. She would train and assist us how to serve in the ministry with her. I knew at that moment the Holy Spirit was speaking to me to Join Apostle Stacie in the prison ministry, this was my confirmation. This is the day that the Lord has made I will rejoice and be glad in it Psalms 118 :24.

I joined Adonai Ministries and walked in the spirit and light. The ministry had a great impact in my life. It opened my eye gates, ear gates and my heart of love. The dark shadowy images in my mind of the prison bars were covered by God's word in *Isaiah 43:2.*
I will never leave you nor forsake you. That scripture came alive in me. Behind the prison bars expect the unexpected. The Challenges ...Yes there were challenges we faced going to the prisons and how God covered us with the blood of Jesus. We saw a bad car accident and we did not stop Apostle Stacie called 911 and we kept it moving. When we entered the prison, we always had to show PROPER ID. One day the guard at the front desk had a bad attitude and was very rude to us.

The guard did not have the correct paperwork for us to enter, the sign in sheets was not in order, dates, and times were not correct and some of our paperwork was lost. We even had misplaced names out of order or not on the list. So, the volunteer coordinator had to be called to the front desk, Apostle Stacie found out she was on vacation, A second call was made to the assistant Chaplin. We proceeded to be searched and a couple were cleared, I just happen that day to be wearing a very expensive Victoria Secret Bra that had an underwire in it. The guard spoke very rudely to me and said I could not enter. I asked could I use his scissors to cut the underwire out my bra, Apostle Stacie spoke up immediately in my defense "this her first time coming with me".

Even as he threw his fiery darts of insults and rudeness, God touched his heart, and I was able to enter the prison with the team. You see God quench all the fiery darts of the wicked because God was with me and was for me that day, and when God is for you who can be against you. But God! No weapon formed against me Shall prosper. Hallelujah! God-made me the head and not the tail, he put me above only and not beneath, God made my enemies my footstool, he made my enemies be at peace with me. Because greater is He that is in me, then he is in the world. After much prayer and intercession, it took the other guard 20 minutes to come chaperone us to the chapel. I was not expecting to see what I saw, the dark shadow and the loud closing of the bars behind us affected me, as we were entering the enemy campgrounds. We were led into the chapel where we would receive the inmates.

The chapel was set up like an auditorium, a stage where we stood, and below was a keyboard and other musical instruments. Apostle Stacie and team set the atmosphere with prayer and praises. A few inmates came to the front below the stage and turned on the music equipment to continue setting the atmosphere, with songs and music as the other inmates entered the chapel singing along. As we began to go into worship Apostle Stacie was introduced, Apostle Stacie spoke the Word that God had given her, she opened the doors to receive God, that Sunday 20 inmates gave their souls to Christ our Savior. Suddenly, I noticed a few inmates from my home city. They were happy to see me and to show me that that some of their lives had been changed.

One of the inmates told me, I wished I had listened to you when I was home in the streets running wild. I lost a few friends in the street and I lost a few friends here, But I gained God Who has changed my life. You see hearing that I know God gave me faith and grace, Adonai's Prison Ministry Impacted my life the 2 years I served under Apostle Stacie leadership and ministry. I learn how to seek the Lord more in quiet times and I learned how to continue stepping out and growing from faith to faith in love, listening and learning how to open my eye gates and ear gates. It was amazing how the spirit of the Lord was moving in the prisons, inmates, and their family's life. The inmates were giving their lives to Christ. I also saw guards change from evil to humbleness before God... the manifestation of God was manifesting right in enemy territory. I saw inmates being set free by the power of the Holy Spirit.

I remember another service when Apostle Stacie was preaching in the men's prison. During altar call one inmate started having a seizure, two inmates rushed over to help him, they knew his medical condition. At that time the guard had stepped out of the chapel, when he returned to the chapel the guard came running down to the inmates with his hand on his gun, he thought they were fighting and he almost pushed the man down button, but the inmate was having a seizure. Thank God he didn't hit the panic button. Two other guards came into the chapel because they heard all the commotion, the paramedics came, and the inmate was taken to hospital. We began to pray and intercede with the inmates for the young man, before we left Apostle Stacie found out the young man was going to be okay... Thank God for his mercy and grace. God got the Glory!

Thank you so much for all that I learned and experienced through Adonai Ministries and the Family is First Project.
Forever grateful,

Linette Allen Ingersoll

THE TESTIMONIALS

Words From the Families and Men Behind Bars

Today, I write these words while looking back on this journey I've been on for some time now. My name is Joseph, and I'm currently incarcerated. I came to know Christ some 9 years ago, and I've totally been transformed since. I've never been afforded the privilege of participating in The Family Is First Project. However, I did get the honor of coming into contact with Apostle Stacie and her team on several occasions here at LORCI for services.

Through Apostle Stacie and her team, I was shown what true liberation looks like, what Kingdom minded men & women of God talk & walk like. Being in here for as long as I have, I've seen a lot of people come into the prisons that meant well but these sistas and brothers came through with that anointing and Good Word! I was always taken in with how they spoke the truth and encouraged us to be who God created us to be. I count it a privileged honor to know them, and to have been a witness of this Kingdom operation. The true showing of what it is to bypass religion and enter into relationship. I salute Apostle Stacie and the whole ministry. I pray that God continues to use them and stretch forth their territory. And I speak against any and all opposition that comes against them.

I speak that in Jesus' Name. I speak furtherance in the ministry, the calling, and the anointing. May we all continue to do the work that Christ has called us to, and may we shine like the cities on a hill that we truly are. I thank the "real ones", they know who they are and then you shall KNOW the Truth, and the Truth shall make you free. Amen.

Bless up.
Joseph

Psalms 37:4 *Delight yourself in the Lord, and he will give you the desires of your heart.:*

* * *

I would like to show my appreciation for The Family is First Project and its founders, Apostle Frank & Stacie Johnson. As five-year participants, my husband and I have been able to learn real relational techniques to build on our communication. My husband and I both are strong personalities, but we learned how to be vulnerable and be open to growth to attain the relationship we both hope to have.

Frank & Stacie Johnson have been transparent with their testimonies, and in return, all of the participating family members and our husbands, sons, brothers, and uncles have been able to relieve ourselves of the burdens we carried concerning incarceration.

We laugh together, and we cry together and no one who comes to this program expecting to learn, and with an open mind, leaves dissatisfied. As a person in ministry myself, I am excited to know that this program is now an option for the women of Dayton Correctional Institution.

May God Bless and Keep You.

LaTesa D. Alumni wife

* * *

My name is Stefanie T, and I am writing you to express my full support for The Family is First Project. Mrs. Johnson has developed and implemented a program that creates transformational change not only in incarcerated individuals, but also in their families. In the beginning of the year, my fiancé, Joshua currently incarcerated at the WCI first approached me about the program. He stated that it was geared towards improving communication between incarcerated individuals and their families. Since I am a very skeptical person by nature, I immediately wondered if the program would have any beneficial impacts on our relationship. Back then, I felt like our communication was already strong and effective. Little did I know that Mrs. Johnson would push us to new limits. During one of the meetings at the prison, Mrs. Johnson asked us to open up about our pasts. She presented us one condition, and the condition was to truly listen to each other. In other words: one person talks, the other person listens.

At first, I thought that this should be a piece of cake. After all, I had been a daughter and sister my entire life. I had taught children for several years, and so, surely, I had listened to others and what they had to say. Listening to others for 15 or 20 minutes without interrupting them is a skill that needs to be learned. Without Mrs. Johnson's facilitation of the conversation, I wouldn't -to this day- know what effective communication really is. I wouldn't know how to listen to another person for 15 minutes straight. I now challenge everyone to ask their loved ones some very deep questions, and to just listen to them.

Not only did The Family is First Project greatly impact our communication skills, but it also gave us the opportunity to meet families that are in similar situations. The support network that The Family is First constitutes is unique in nature, and I know a lot of families who now continue to offer each other emotional support. To sum it up, I would love to see The Family Is First Project not only continued at WCI, but also expanded to other institutions. It transforms incarcerated individuals and their families in that it gives them tools to communicate effectively and to lean on each other for support.

Kind regards,
Stefanie- Girlfriend

* * *

Hello, my name is Gladys. I had a son, Antonio, who was incarcerated. Mrs. Stacie Johnson was such an asset in Our Lives. Her program The Family is First Project, helped him (and me) to break down the barriers that sometimes can be created when a loved one goes to jail. She spoke with family members of the inmates, and we (family members), met on the outside for group meetings, financial burden's, getting to know our incarcerated loved one's all over again, as well as being able to discuss Anything we were going through. Mrs. Johnson was also able to have group gatherings

INSIDE the prison facilities, where raw emotions were unveiled, and fathers were reconnected with their sons. She is such a Blessing to ANY inmate/family member that she has come in contact with!!!! Had it not been for this truly Blessed Woman, I'm not sure what we would have done.

I wish she could go to ALL the Correctional Facilities in Ohio, because she is a wonderful person spiritually, physically, and emotionally! I Love her commitment to this Program!!!! My son and I still talk about her, to this day. He was unable to continue to participate in her program because he was moved to LECI, where she has been unable to develop The Family Is First Project. I pray that she will be able to place her program throughout all Ohio, because she possesses a wonderful gift within her!! I appreciate this Woman's commitment to this awesome program and my son, and my son and I were truly blessed to be part of it.

Kindest Regards,
Gladys P Alumni Mother

* * *

First off, I want to say thank you to the gentleman that suggested my son to get involved with the Family's First Program. My son has been incarcerated for 6 years now and is serving a double life sentence. It was devastating to me and my family. I felt that there was no one out there to talk to that would understand what I was going thru. The Family's First Project has helped me and my son tremendously; without this program I would still be where I was 6 years ago, feeling alone. Just knowing that you are not alone in this world and that there is someone out there going thru this same situation. This program has shown me how to cope and deal with my son being incarcerated. Just having someone to talk to that knows how it feels to have someone incarcerated is a blessing.

When my son started in this program he was just going thru the motions, and we didn't think he was going to be able to complete it. But this program has changed him to where he is a different person; it has shown him how to cope and how to deal with his anger. Also, you are getting to know other families that are going thru the same stuff that I am, and it is nice to be able to talk to other people. I just want to thank Pastor Stacie Johnson for the Family's First Program and helping me and my son in dealing with his incarceration. When I first came to the first meeting, I sat and cried thru the whole thing because everything Pastor Johnson said, that was me.

I was blaming myself but as time went on, I started to get stronger and stronger, and I no longer cried. I just want to say again that I am so thankful for The Family Is First Project. I am looking forward to my son graduating. This is the first program he has been involved in and because of Family First he has participated in many other programs. I just once again want to say thank you to Pastor Stacie Johnson for the Family's First Program.

Sincerely, Sherelle (Mother)

* * *

First, let me say that it is and was a blessing to meet and work with Apostle Stacie as she is a fully invested worker for the uplifting and reintegration of offenders and ex-offenders. She has helped my family keep our son on track and alive while incarcerated and gave us an opportunity to reiterate to him things we taught and he ignored, to his demise. He has grown up tremendously over the last nine years and truly has come to understand his role and position in life. As his father, I had a chance to talk to him again about things we discussed, and he admitted a clearer understanding and regret for his arrogance. Qa'id has participated in counseling for himself and services for others. He coordinated several prison programs and lowered his status which afforded him the opportunity to be moved to a less restricted prison environment.

Now he serves others by acting as a medic transport person. Through the exposure and participation in "The Family Is First Program," Qa'id has been encouraged to take a realistic self-evaluation of his life … of his past, present and future. Both inmates and loved ones have learned how to relax and share their troubling thoughts. This program allows all the participants to have a safe and trusting environment for a heartfelt conversation. The program is scripted and guided by Pastor Stacie Johnson. Pastor Johnson sets the tone for the inmates and loved ones to speak freely and to feel safe enough to want to share their deep thoughts and deepest feelings.

Since we became members of The Family Is First Project, we have witnessed a healing between family and other loved ones; my family was a recipient of this blessing. Apostle Stacie has used her own life experiences and has inspired others to reach out and forgive each other. By exposing the test in their lives and keeping God First, I feel that this program needs to be repeated in every prison in the USA, and abroad. I am sure it is needed and can help others as it has done for my family, and so many others.

Sincerely,

Yusuf and Gwen Aqueelah (Alumni parents)

* * *

My name is Bruce and I attended the Family is First Project ran by Apostle Stacie Johnson for approximately 3 years. My first year was as a student. I learned how to reinforce my relationship with my loved ones and friends while being locked up. My next 2 years was as an alumni facilitator.

During that time, I continued to learn and grow through the topics discussed. The whole process of the Family is First Project is to strengthen the bond between an inmate and his family or friend who has a short amount of time or an inmate who may not even be going home. By keeping bonds strong between friends and loved ones, it enables the inmate to keep his eye on the prize as well as eases the stress on his family. I am truly grateful for the opportunity to have taken this program as it has helped me grow as a man. I am also grateful for Ms. Johnson's devotion and dedication to making a difference in people's lives for she is truly doing the Lord's work.

Thank you for your time.
Bruce S (Alumni inmate)

* * *

Dear Apostle Stacie Johnson, first and foremost, I thank you. I remember how you helped me grow mentally, physically, and spiritually. The Family Is First Project help me along with my loved ones how to not become a burden while being incarcerated.

To learn how to manage your financial means without hurting your loved ones. It helps your family to understand that there are other families who have the same hurt that they have, and to actually see that it's not just them by their self. To hear other people, speak about the hurt and pain that their incarcerated loved one has caused them, but they just didn't know how to tell them. It's an amazing experience, and I recommend it for anyone who is doing time with or without a loved one.

Thanks,
Donate (Alumni inmate)

* * *

The Family Is First Project has had a huge impact on my life. It is because this program, and powerful Apostle Stacie Johnson, that I have a better relationship with my family, and that I am able to live a productive life while I'm in prison. Not only did The Family Is First Project open my understanding on how to have a healthy relationship while I'm incarcerated, but it also helped me to be a better man. I've learned how to establish boundaries, and before my relationship with family could grow, I had to uproot the cause of the pain and resentment. During this class, my family and I have become closer, and I have gained their level of trust and we moved to a place in our relationship where we can have honest communication. We learned the difference between conversation and communication.

My perspective has matured, and I gained life lesson[s] being a part of the Family Is First Project. I am capable of making productive decisions now and know how to handle situations I am faced with. Truthfully, my life has improved, and because of the time and effort Apostle Stacie Johnson has not only put into the class, but into individuals, my relationship with my loved ones has enhanced…....I'm grateful and honored to have been a part of the Family Is First Project…....

Marcus J (Alumni inmate)

* * *

Dear Apostle Stacie, The Family Is First Project had a very positive impact on my life; I am speaking truth. I am so very grateful for you and your program in my life. Because of you, my relationship with my family is growing stronger. Just last month, I heard from one of my brothers for the first time in almost 20 years. It was due to the building I have been doing with the family you met in the program. Life with my family is so much better. Thanks again for that initial guidance; your mentorship was nothing but a gift from GOD preparing me for greater works. I am obedient, faithful, and ready. I am a member of Toastmasters now and I have completed my Icebreaker. I know I am on my way to becoming that motivational speaker.

Take care and GOD bless you!
Patrick (inmate)

* * *

Apostle Stacie,

I just wanted to thank you for all the work you do and helping to set up programs like the one we had today. Please send my best regards to your husband. His word was right on time and I'm not sure if you were able to see or not, but God was definitely doing some molding in my life and was breaking some things off my life...that's why I got so choked up when he asked me to recite the bible verse regarding thinking like a child and acting like a child. Standing in front of that group of people the Holy Spirit grabbed a hold of me and as began reciting the gospel it was so powerful, I couldn't barely contain myself. I'm sorry for rambling just please send my best to your husband and let him know his message didn't fall on deaf ears.

Thanks, Dustin (inmate)

* * *

The Family Is First Project clearly made me a more effective communicator. As a result of this program, I was able to gain trust with my family. A lot of information was withheld from me because of my immature mind set. By me being consistent with attending class, I have now been empowered to lead and provide encouragement to family and also fellow inmates. As of now I look back and see how everyone in the class is growing. I mean nobody stayed the same. People who did not speak at all are now speaking in public, boldly. Guys who had a hard time understanding the role of a real man is no longer lost and confused. I will never forget that a man is a protector, the provider, and one who holds strength. I can strongly say this program has given me hope; it reminded me that I still have a purpose.

I have opportunities to operate in my gift. (Nov.7) In closing, I will like to end with a Quick testimony. I've been locked up going on eight years for a murder I did not do. I could of thrown in the towel years ago, meaning, giving up; this class gave me an expectation. I knew I was here for a purpose. NOW GOD IS MOVING IN MY SITUATION LIKE NEVER BEFORE. MY CODEFENDENT who lied on me is now taking back his statement. In that's all I needed for a new trial. When I actually come home, I want to help out with The Family Is First Project. Free of charge...amen

Best Regards,

Charles (Alumni inmate)

* * *

My name is Merrell I am incarcerated and I'm a part of The Family Is First Project. This program has truly helped me. I've learned more in this program than I've ever learned on the streets. Being in this program has really opened my eyes to the hurt and pain I've brought to my family and even myself. This program also blessed my growth process in life; before this program I didn't know how to be a father, son, brother, husband, friend or a man; but now I can say that I am everything I said above because of the time, patience, wisdom and genuine love Pastor Stacie Johnson has put into me as a person and us as a program/family. I got 15 years but I can get out early in the year 2020, and just having that time puts a lot of stress on me, my children, my mom, and my fiancé, and we started to let the stress and sadness take over our lives but when I got my family involved in this program it was like "man we got to get each other back on track" cause we are all we got, and family means everything. We've learned how to put everything in GOD'S hands and just walk in faith. I am grateful that Pastor Johnson stuck with me through all my mishaps and all my difficulties, she still made sure that I became the man I am today and my life will never be the same because now I know I deserve better than the streets and jail, and that I know my children deserves more out of me. They don't deserve not having me there. This program is a HUGE part of my life and forever will it be.

I would advise anybody who needs help mending, any family relationships that needs help molding, this is the program for them. This program is for the real so if you fake and you don't like to hear the real about life or yourself then I don't know what to tell you cause with this program, it's about growth, and that's what really going to give you, growth! Forever will I appreciate this program. I truly love it with all of my heart and for anyone who joins the next class be ready cause it's going to get real. Thank you and GOD BLESS!

Respectfully,
Merrell (inmate)

* * *

Dear Apostle Stacie, The Family Is First Project not only helped my marriage, it assisted it. Not only did it strengthen my marriage and family relationships, The Family Is First Project exposed it. When I say expose, I mean it truly allowed me to see and detect where in all places the little foxes were spoiling my vines.

As head of my house even from prison there were a lot of things had to re-learn that I really, really thought I knew. As a Man of God, teacher, Life-Coach, and Husband, I came to realize my communication had to change when it came to communicating with my wife. It is often very hard to reveal all that's screaming inside of you to be trusted and loved when you are from a Lifestyle of Major Hustling. I had to first know within myself that the transformation back from Tone, Tone to Antonio was true and regardless of who ride and don't ride, I must become a cleaner, more pure responsible me.

And, prior to The Family is First Project, I thought I was there, but The Family is First Project ultimately assisted me in not only getting there, but in becoming the Lead Co-Facilitator who assisted many, many other men and their families in getting there. I could go on and on, but I won't; but I will end by saying that THERE IS NOTHING THAT SCREAMS GENTLEMAN OR LADY MORE THAN A MAN OR A WOMAN WHO LIVES THE ART OF PLACING IN Proper perspective his or her family, Wife, Husband, boyfriend, or girlfriend FIRST! May Gods hand be forever on your life so that people like me can not only feel it but experience it. God Bless.

Respectfully,

Antonio (Alumni- inmate)

* * *

The Family is First Project is excellent in finding and repairing the broken points in any relationship. I've learned the fundamentals of healthy communication and I've received the tools to maintain my family relationships through hardships. I would recommend this program to any family of an incarcerated person even if you believe that your relationship is strong and healthy.

Pat (inmate)

* * *

The Family is First Project is a program that strengthens the bonds of family. The program provides participants the chance to see where they are strong in their relationships and where they are weak. The foundation of this opportunity is also blended with the support of the Word of God.

Apostle Stacie, creator and facilitator of the Family is First Project challenges the class to look deep within themselves and realize of they have errors in their thinking. Once she has awakened her students to where they need to improve, she then works with the families, so they know the proper way to support their loved ones while incarcerated. After she has sharpened everyone's skills, she brings them together to show how much more effective their communication can be with one another.

The Family is First Project is a program I would highly recommend. Unlike state offered programs where some facilitators don't truly care about results, Mrs. Johnson has walked in our shoes which gave birth to this program, and she cares to see other people teaching them not to experience what she had to endure. The Family is First Project gave my family and me an opportunity to grow together; we have never had in 18 years. This program is one every inmate should be an alumni of.

Jeff (inmate)

* * *

When I first signed up for The Family is First Project, I didn't know what to expect. I figured that it was going to be a lot of fun; since I finally had someone in my life that was going to go through this experience with me. For the guys that are in here. Our very first meeting Pastor Johnson gave us an application to fill out and we had to write a short essay. I wasn't prepared for the work it was going to take to get to know my family who I thought I already knew.

During the course of last year, I have grown so much with my woman. Through each family meeting, the honesty, and transparency that she shared with me has made our relationship more intimate than ever. My relationship with my mother, which I always thought was pretty good, became better.

Sometimes when we mean well to our family; but sometimes we can take unconditional love for granted. What Family First showed me was what they went through. The Family is First Project was the platform for them to finally express that to me. I never knew how strong they were being for me. This experience has humbled me and gave me the gratitude that I needed to honor my family. I was able to have church with my woman in prison. She was able to see how I praised and worshiped my Lord and Savior Jesus Christ.

The Pastor Stacie prayed over us. To see the tears come down her eyes; has been a moment that has been frozen in time in my mind. I hope and pray that all of you who have family members incarcerated can go through the Family is First Project experience. With love and respect,
Alonzo

* * *

Incarceration with no relationship with the outside world is a very depressing case. I was just an ordinary inmate when I first joined The Family is First Project, with the intent of hoping to learn something. at first, I thought I had a great relationship with my family and that everything is all aces. Only to find out that there are some things that needed to be worked on in my relationship with my family including repairing communications, attitude and also understanding that I have to learn how to be responsible in my thoughts and actions.

But first, I must admit that change is needed, and I must allow it to happen. During these classes I was able to grow in some areas I needed growth in, and also, I needed to have the opportunity to talk about intimate things that I won't talk about on regular visits. As the classes proceeded, I started to see changes in my life. I wasn't an inmate anymore, but I became a man, true to my word myself and my actions. A mentor to others who looked up to me and they seen the change in me and the desires to change. My improvement spurred out until it was noticed by Apostle Stacie Johnson.

She decided to make me a part of her alumni and that opened doors for me to be able to encourage other guys who wished to change and understand that life is not a playground. I am a third year Alumni and I have grown extremely well. Thanks to The Family is First Project. if you are reading this, always understand that in life there are obstacles and circumstances beyond control and even though it might be the results or outcome of our past actions, don't forget that change is around the corner waiting to be embraced. but you have to recognize it and give it a chance and God will guide you through that change by sending you the right person to help you just like he did me. recognize change today and give it a chance.

Sam O (Alumni Inmate)

* * *

Apostle Stacie, this program helps many make time easier for their families and themselves. You have done an amazing job and you and your husband are a great success. You and your husband are an inspiration for many. You two show many that husbands and wives can make it thru a prison term.

Jason (Alumni inmate)

* * *

I have been taking courses and classes for over 20 yrs. in prison. To be honest most of these were for the parole board. I went to the board in 2008 and was given a lot more time and was told "programs don't change what you did." So, I had not taken a class since and was sure not to UNLESS it was for me. So, I was told of The Family Is First Project, and since I am married to a strong Christian woman who has had my back for so long, I felt we needed this program or to at least try the course and see if it had anything in it to help us as a family. I didn't expect much and ended up getting so much out of this program and it helped tighten the bond between my wife and me, and it let us see the other person's point of view a bit more. So, if a class can do that for a couple when the man has been in prison well over 20 years it has to be a great thing and seen as a blessing. I'd encourage anyone with any family members still trying to hang on to take the class.

You will get something out of it to help YOUR ENTIRE family and isn't that what we as men are looking for? Some type of help for those helping us. My favorite saying I heard and I'm uncertain of who said it but..."You do what you care about and make an excuse for the rest." That says it all for my family!!

Thank you very much.

Matthew P (Alumni Inmate)

* * *

My testimony: I was a non-believer in this program and was very optimistic about everything that could happen or be taught. As a man serving a 30 to life sentence you would imagine most people would give up on life and yes, I was one of many who wanted to give up. Through trials and tribulation and losing 3 of the most important people in my life it has been more than a challenge. Keep this in mind I was a devoted Muslim for 14 years but in all my years of praying to Allah I have never received an answer for my many of prayers... The Family is First Project taught me how to recognize I wasn't the man I thought. Apostle Stacie Johnson and the other members of The Family is First Project helped me in ways that I don't really have enough time to explain. But one day I was in need of peace so I tried to pray to "Jesus Christ" and from that day forth my prayers were answered and from that prayer I have never felt a better peace in my life.

Remember, you are listening to a 14-year devoted Muslim to a now born-again follower of Christ. Don't get me wrong there are some kinks to still be worked out, but I can tell you if this program doesn't do anything for you or your family that means neither of you tried.

I have found honor, joy, peace, love and a new family through perfect strangers all because I chose to open up my life and my heart to something new...God will always forgive; even if you curse him out, he knows the pain and the struggle before you go through it but all you have to do is believe.

GOD BLESS... KEVIN. (Alumni Inmate)

* * *

About Author

Stacie Johnson is an inspirational speaker and change agent. She is known for her motivational, life changing, explosive style of speaking. She displays realness and compassion as she encourages and motivates others.

Stacie is a transformational speaker who has the ability to touch any individual no matter their walk of life. She has spent most of her professional journey as a life coach, facilitator, and corrections specialist. She provides a holistic and spiritual touch as she empowers women and men across the nation.

Stacie is the founder of Women of Vision Global Network. This powerful women's network was created as a safe platform for women to network, develop a real sisterhood, celebrate each other, discuss their issues, speak their truth, and tap into their gifts, talents, and resources as they pursue their God given purpose. She and her husband Frank are the founders of Adonai Ministries, and The Family is First Project, a prison ministry that breaks down the barriers of communication and deals with the unhealthy lifestyle choices of those incarcerated, and their families.

Stacie Johnson has been recognized for her outstanding volunteer work in the community and prisons. In 2015. Stacie was commissioned as a Kentucky Colonel by Governor Steven Beshear, which is the highest title of honor bestowed by the Governor of Kentucky. Stacie has also been awarded the prestigious Phenomenal Woman Award by the One Accord Women's Ministry of New Beginnings Community Church.

Stacie Johnson is a certified Chemical Dependency Counselor Assistant (CDCA II), Certified Life Coach and she has also obtained her certificate as a publisher. Stacie has earned her Bachelor of Science in Criminal Justice from The University of Phoenix, and a Master's in Human Services with a concentration in Non-Profit Management from The University of the Rockies. Stacie is currently obtaining her Doctorate in Organizational Development and Leadership from Grand Canyon University.

Professionally, Stacie has held positions such as CEO, Director, Team Lead, Clinical Case Manager, Re-entry Outreach Coordinator and Para Counselor. She continues to work closely with the Mental Health Board, and she works closely with children and families who suffer from behavior and mental disabilities.

Her profound understanding of behavior patterns and knowledge of emotional and psychological patterns has allowed her to act as a consultant, advocating for families and women who deserve another chance at life and to be heard. Her professional skills consistently ensure long-term viability as she continues to address unhealthy behaviors and attitudes of individuals while assisting them in transforming their lives through positive influence and healthy collaboration. Stacie Johnson is a mother of four, grandmother of five, and lives in Cincinnati, Ohio with her husband Frank.

STACIE L. JOHNSON

References

Revised Standard Version (RSV)
New American Standard Bible (NASB)
New Life Version (NLV)
New King James Version (NKJV)
Merriam-Webster Online Dictionary
Dr. Tony Evans (Kingdom Man Book
https://www.biblestudy.org/bibleref/meaning-of-numbers-in-bible/
Roy T. Bennett (Quote)
William Glasser (Quote)
Candice Bure (Quote)
Henry Ford (Quote)

STACIE JOHNSON BOOKS AND EBOOKS

While you Wait is a book that will change the game! It's an eye opener to the hidden truths about the impact and emotional stressors of loving someone behind bars. Stacie waited 10 years while her husband was incarcerated; through her journey, she unveils the stories of many women today who take on the role of the caregiver. Through her book **While You Wait** you will learn how to cope with incarceration, the financial struggle, feelings of shame, the weight of responsibility, all while developing a deeper prayer life in the midst of waiting.

First things first, I want to congratulate you on this achievement. I know that this book was your baby, and you see it all grown up. I'm just in awe because I didn't know what to expect. This book was written for a woman-based audience; but as a man, it was also helpful for me. Not only was it inspirational but it was kind of like a prison survival guide.

You were teaching along with sharing your journey which makes your book so powerful. You exposed a lot of things people go through that are left unsaid. Everyone who goes through the prison system, whether it's an inmate or supporter, experiences your journey in some way at some point. So, I thank you for exposing your struggles and I hope that this book has great success. I also thank those who helped you in making this book a masterpiece. I'm eager to read your future books.

Book review by Derick Patterson

An Unveiled Heart is **Soul Stirring**!

Apostle Stacie Johnson's "An Unveiled Heart" is one of the most Prolific, Powerful, and Compelling Books Ever Read. From the First Chapter **" The Elect Ladies**" to the Final Chapter, **" It's Time to Hit The Reset Button** She Opens Up and Speaks With Such A Pure Honesty from the depths of her Soul about Her own Painful but Powerful Journey of Self Discovery and Self Love!

Boldly and Unapologetically, she peels back the intricate layers and unravels the myths and self- destroying mechanisms we impose on ourselves as well as those we allow to come into our lives to derail and destroy our hopes and dreams.

She talks candidly about the devastation of not feeling good enough...loving yet not being loved, low self-esteem, and the dangerous effects of co-dependency. Stacie exposes the catastrophic and detrimental untruths, deceptions, and false expectations that can and will devastate our lives, preventing us from ever reaching our full potential in life.

Book review by Dr. Pamela Robinson, PSY. D, DNP, DVS and Certified Life & Health Coach

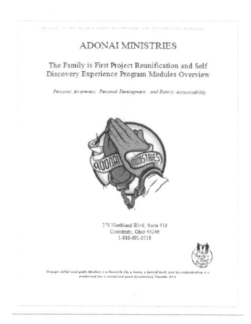

The Family is First Project training workbook provides a holistic approach to coping with being a part of the prison system. Through bible-based education and training, The Family Is First Project addresses many of the challenges faced by families and their incarcerated loved ones. By being a support system for the aforementioned population, this workbook helps encourage healthy community interactions and builds collaborative relationships with people of like vision. This workbook is perfect for focus group and self-development classes within and without the prison walls. It also helps address the issues of family relationships. This is a transformational self-discovery, family reunification experience that will ensure **rehabilitation** within the prison and community.

Made in the USA
Monee, IL
13 May 2022